The Graviton *of* God

The celestial wonders and statistical
impossibilities of our universe,
bodies, and existence.

Dr. James Kindlund

WESTBOW
PRESS®
A DIVISION OF THOMAS NELSON
& ZONDERVAN

WestBow Press books may be ordered through booksellers or by contacting:

WestBow Press
A Division of Thomas Nelson & Zondervan
1663 Liberty Drive
Bloomington, IN 47403
www.westbowpress.com
844-714-3454

All Scripture quotations are taken from The Holy Bible, New International Version®, NIV® Copyright © 1973, 1978, 1984, 2011 by Biblica, Inc.® Used by permission. All rights reserved worldwide.

ISBN: 978-1-6642-1020-2 (sc)
ISBN: 978-1-6642-1022-6 (hc)
ISBN: 978-1-6642-1021-9 (e)

Library of Congress Control Number: 2020921074

Print information available on the last page.

WestBow Press rev. date: 10/28/2020

This book is dedicated to:

The Creator of the Universe and my family.

Contents

Introduction

I was sitting in cellular and molecular biology class at the University of Miami, circa 2009. The professor was discussing the proteins involved in deoxyribonucleic acid (DNA) replication. I then began to ponder the question, what came first, the protein or the DNA? For protein is needed to unwind the DNA and then other proteins are needed to begin replicating the DNA, but DNA is a set of coding instructions for ... protein! I then became fascinated with the complexities of life and what were the statistical chances that life began randomly. And even when it did begin, how did it know how to evolve in the way that it did? How is it that complex molecules not only came together randomly but were also completely functional? Not only that, these molecules must be encased in a safe environment, i.e. a cellular wall. Albumin, the most abundant protein in the human bloodstream would degrade if left out in the open world.

This journey led to eleven years of studying intelligent design and evolution. Comparing the validity of each. This book intends to demonstrate the statistical unlikelihood of macroevolution. An example of macroevolution is a fish eventually becoming a horse. This is different from microevolution that entails species making adaptations to their environment. Examples of this are changing color of fur for camouflage, reproducing asexually (self-reproduction), or bacteria developing resistance to antibiotics for survival.

I would humbly ask that even the staunchest Darwinists who

read this book, who think of themselves as intellectuals, read and appreciate the validity of what is entailed in this book. Science should not have sides, but macroevolution is far from settled science. We are made of trillions of cells and trillions of microorganisms (tiny living creatures) that live symbiotically with us. We are far more complex than the stars in the galaxy. Humans consist of twenty different types of active atoms/elements whereas the Earth's sun is mostly made of just one atom, hydrogen. Scientists, though, have identified as many as sixty chemical elements in the human body but remain unsure of what purpose they all serve.

We and many other animals consist of tens of thousands of different types of proteins, each needing its own genetic code. Even the most basic of organisms (living things), bacteria, require somewhere between 265 and 350 protein-producing genes at minimum to survive! So, what are the chances of a single protein (a molecule that carries out a task) randomly coming together and working perfectly, let alone 265 proteins? We must also consider the thousands of genes necessary to carry the instructions for producing these proteins. Human DNA consists of 3 billion base pairs with at least 30,000 genes.

All of this coupled with the fact that the Earth is the perfect size for life, Earth's tilt is crucial for life, as is the size of our moon, as well as the size and type of our Sun. Earth is located in an almost perfect celestial location for the creation and maintenance of life but also for observing and studying our universe. An example being the sun is 400 times larger than the moon but also 400 times further away, hence why we can study solar eclipses perfectly or the fact that we live in a very well organized and 'clean' solar system and galaxy that enables us to see extremely far into the universe. Amongst the minimum 100 billion stars of our Milky Way galaxy we are in a most fortuitous location.

This text will go through the physical and biological aspects of our existence. Some of the statistical evidence of this book is to be applied to later chapters for full appreciation. For instance, the statistical odds listed in chapter three should be referenced while reading chapters four through six because the core equations of the mathematical phenomenon that is life are attained within. There is a cumulative effect. The reader should recall the incredible astrological and physical odds and ponder it, even while reading about the clotting cascade. Because not only must one consider what is being discussed but also the fact that it is occurring in an almost impossible location in the universe, with nearly improbable physical parameters.

So, sit back, relax, and prepare for a journey into the phenomenon that is our existence …

PART I

THE PHYSICAL FACTS

One

THE CALCULABLE COSMOS

You stare up in the sky on a clear fall evening. The stars of the heavens are magnificent, gorgeous even. What if I told you the happenings of the cells inside your body are far more complex and spectacular than the stars in the universe? However, for life to exist it needs a home on which to live.

The big bang is the accepted scientific explanation for the creation of the universe. The term big bang is a bit of a misnomer as it is thought to be many explosions occurring simultaneously. The theory still maintains there is a beginning point or epicenter with an ever-expanding universe. And thus, the stars were born, as well as *every single* piece of matter. Stars are the source of many of the elements of our universe, mostly the heavy elements such as carbon and iron. These heavy elements are synthesized in the core of stars. They are dispersed amongst the universe during the explosion of a star—called a supernova.

The great mysteries begin immediately. The obvious question being, how did the big bang begin? We will leave this question to the epilogue. The mystery is expanded by the production of the light elements such as deuterium (an isotope of hydrogen) and helium. An isotope is simply that element with a different number of neutrons in its nucleus (core). The light elements could not have formed from stars because, believe it or not, you would need temperatures in the billions of degrees Fahrenheit in order to synthesize these elements. So how were they formed?

The mysterious universe is also finely tuned. The United States of America put men on the moon using a rudimentary computer equivalent in computing power to some modern calculators. How is this possible? Because the symmetry of the universe is so consistent it renders it very calculable. There are now more than thirty identified parameters that need to be in place in order for life to exist. So how finely tuned is the universe?

The cosmological constant is the energy density of space. Just this one variable's constant is thought to be fine-tuned to the one part in a 10^{53}. That is fifty-three zeros! A trillion is twelve zeros. This number is truly incomprehensible for the human mind. We can visualize it on paper but to truly comprehend a statistic of this size is difficult. To help paint a picture of the odds of this, it would be the same as hitting a target with a dart that is one trillionth of a trillionth of an inch in diameter. One physical parameter down, twenty-nine to go.

For the universe to exist it requires hydrogen (the smallest of the atoms) to be converted to helium. This is accomplished by nuclear fusion. Specifically, it must convert $7/1000^{th}$ of its mass. If $6/1000^{th}$ of its mass was converted, then no transformation would take place. If $8/1000^{th}$ of its mass was converted, then bonding would be so prolific that the hydrogen supply of the universe would be exhausted. Hydrogen has one proton in its nucleus. It is sometimes referred to as just "proton" (see graph 1 below). There are an estimated 10,000 ,000,000,000,000,000,000,000,000,000,000,000,000,000,000,0 00,000,000,000,000,000,000,000,000,000 or ten to the 79th power (10^{79}) protons in the universe.

All these protons had to be created at the same time. The first law of physics states that matter can neither be created nor destroyed, thus none of these protons can disappear. A "law" in science is exceedingly rare because it means it is true 100 percent of the time.

A *hypothesis* is a possible explanation and a *theory* essentially means us scientists are pretty sure it is correct.

The second law of thermodynamics states that entropy (disorganization or chaos) either stays the same or increases. The entropy of the universe can never decrease. Thus, everything should be moving toward disorganization, and the energy of the universe should be decreasing. Life is highly organized and seems to decrease entropy. Living things turn disorder (molecules) into order (life).

This law in recent decades has been reworded to fit the atheist scientist's narrative. The moment proponents of intelligent design jumped on the discrepancy, they were quick to twist the explanation of how life can be squeezed to fit within the second law of thermodynamics. Part of their argument is to state that life is not a closed system but an open one, which receives energy to maintain its system. Even if that point is accepted, it still means the first organisms to have ever existed needed to defy this law of physics.

The subparticles (pieces) of an atom are neutrons, protons, and electrons. The protons and neutrons are at the center of the atom—known as the nucleus—while electrons circle around the nucleus of the atom like swarming bees. Atoms are the smallest particles that exist of which everything is made of. Two or more atoms joining together is called a molecule. It is in the molecule form that the vast majority of chemical reactions and functions take place.

Atoms stick together via their electron clouds. To put it simply, they share electrons. Na^+ is a single atom of sodium, and Cl^- is a single atom of chloride, and $NaCl$ are the two atoms together, called a molecule, specifically sodium chloride, also known as table salt. Nuclear fusion (atoms fusing together) inside of stars require neutrons and protons to be a certain distance from one another. Protons have a slightly greater mass than neutrons. If one were to increase the distance between the neutrons and protons inside the atoms of the stars by just a factor of $1/700^{th}$, nuclear fusion would cease. No nuclear fusion, no stars. No stars, no Sun—and no Sun, no life on Earth. There is an undeniable harmony and symmetry of the universe. One would expect far more chaos to exist in the universe, especially if explosions are occurring all over the place. Why are such precise events taking place?

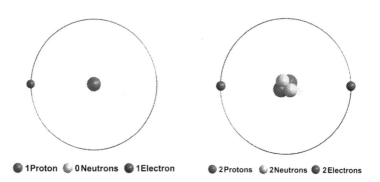

1Proton 0Neutrons 1Electron   2Protons 2Neutrons 2Electrons

[**Graph 1: Left**: *The Hydrogen atom. One proton, no neutron, and one electron. Sometimes referred to as a "Proton" since it only has one proton in its nucleus.* **Right**: *Helium has two protons, two neutrons, and two electrons. All atoms of the periodic table have all three components of an atom with hydrogen being the only exception.*]

A long-toted notion of atheists is that our plant, solar system, and Sun are nothing special. We are just a fleck of dust in the universe. However, if one were to study the matter more closely and without biases, one begins to understand the unique nature of these entities. I do not blame them, no one educated them on the uniqueness of our existence. Facts of our galaxy and solar system are not refuted by atheist astrologists, they just seem to never make it into our primary and secondary school textbooks.

We are, in all actuality, very well placed in our galaxy. Our galaxy, the Milky Way, like most galaxies, is a terrifying place of asteroids, comets, and exploding stars everywhere. The highest volume of exploding stars are in the center of the galaxy. The Milky Way has spirals coming from the center that make our galaxy look as if it is in a washing machine. The spirals are also areas of giant molecular clouds and supernovae (star explosions). Our solar system, just happens to be in a galactic "safe zone." It is free of these supernovae and massive molecular clouds. Where there are more stars exploding. There are more heavy elements. However, if the solar system were too close to the center the radiation would make us as desolate as Mars. Too far away and there are not enough heavy elements for life to utilize. As I write this, I see an amateur scientific website call our place in the Milky Way boring. However, it is precisely this spot in the Milky Way that allows life to flourish. We do not have to be the center of the galaxy—and trust me—you do not want to be there.

Even the shape of our galaxy is conducive to having an Earth-like planet. As stated, we have a spiral galaxy. The thinness of our disc-shaped galaxy assures that our Sun stays in its desirable circular orbit, and being circular helps keep us in the safe zone.

Another type of galaxy is the elliptical galaxy. These galaxies have stars in random orbits. Could you imagine living in a galaxy where stars are in random orbits? Earth would be pulled this way at one point in time and that way at another point in time. The Earth's temperatures would fluctuate from frigid to scorching wasteland depending on which star the Earth was orbiting and its distance from it. The stars in the elliptical galaxy are less dense and thus lack the heavy metals necessary to create a planet like Earth and the life that inhabit it.

Then there are the irregular galaxies. These galaxies are even worse. They are distorted, ripping apart, and have stars exploding throughout it. Could you imagine Earth trying to exist in this type of galaxy? Oh, and that boring galaxy of ours? It is in the top two percent most massive and brilliantly luminous of all known galaxies.

The Sun

Now let us focus into our solar system that include the Sun and eight planets. The Sun is the driving force for all of the energy for life on Earth. It provides energy to the plants, algae, and phytoplankton that in turn give off oxygen. Then we animals breathe this oxygen. Again, I have heard over and over again that our Sun is "boring" or "nothing special." What if I told you our Sun is in the top ten percent most massive star types in the universe? What if I told you it is in a class of only three and a half percent of all known stars in the universe? Well, I would be telling you the truth. Not only that, the size of the Earth and our distance from the Sun allows our life supporting temperatures to occur.

The vast majority of stars are red dwarfs. Just for reference, our Sun is colloquially called a yellow dwarf. The Sun's real classification is a G-type main-sequence star or G2V. Okay, take it easy, Spock. The red dwarfs are much smaller than the Sun and not hot enough to sustain life as we know it on Earth. And by hot enough, I am inferring to how much ultraviolet radiation they produce. You need an x amount of ultraviolet radiation to split water molecules in order to build oxygen levels up in the atmosphere. There also must be a certain level of ultraviolet light or radiation to split carbon dioxide, so the plant can use the carbon portion to grow and release the oxygen for us and other animals to breathe.

Well, what if you just moved us closer to a smaller sun? This would not work either due to a physical influence known as tidal force. This is the force between a star and its planet. As a planet nears their star the rotation of the planet slows, if close enough, the planet stops spinning all together. Again, this would result with two sides of the Earth with polar differences in temperatures and light. Too wild to sustain life or for a growing season. It has been estimated that if Earth were just three to five percent closer to the Sun, we would be a desolate wasteland like Mars. If Earth were three to five percent further away from the Sun, it would be a barren ice land, much like the dark side of Venus. At 77.7 miles (125 kilometers) above the planet's surface, Venus's weather is -283° F (-175 °C) with a good chance of carbon dioxide ice. How can a planet, far closer to the Sun than Earth, be so cold? One factor is Venus's thin atmospheric content, but because Venus rotates so slowly (tidal force), the dark side of Venus gets extremely cold. Venus's equator rotates at 4.05 mph (6.52 km/h), whereas Earth's rotates at 1,040.4 mph (1,674.4 km/h). In addition to this, if Earth were orbiting an F-type dwarf, as compared with our G-type dwarf Sun, the ozone (O_3) levels would be far too high, and oxygen dependent life would die off.

Then there are the more massive stars. The bigger, the better right? Normal philosophy for America, deadly philosophy for life to exist. For one, massive stars do not live that long. Many massive stars are actually in their later stages of life and are getting ready to explode. Even a star just slightly larger star than our own Sun would only live a few billion years. Oh, not to mention Earth would be destroyed by the massive amount of heat. The Sun is a nice 9,932° F (5,500°C) while some of the more massive stars are upwards of 71,540° F (39,727 ° C). Their luminosity is up to 1,000,000 times that of our Sun. Imagine the sunglasses needed to protect your eyes from that. The Sun is already 4.6 billion years old, not to mention it is rich in heavy metals and is very stable. The ultraviolet output of the Sun varies by only $\frac{1}{10}$ of one percent over a full Sun cycle or roughly eleven years. This stability prevents wild shifts in the Earth's climate. A stable climate is a predictable climate and a predictable climate is ideal for growing food and knowing when to harvest. Replace the Sun with any other type of star in the known universe and life could not exist on Earth.

The Moon and Planets

The Moon? Really? The Moon. The moon is responsible for helping the Earth? I thought it was just a hunk of rock floating in Earth's orbit? Yes! Firstly, our moon is unique in that it is very large for a moon. Relative to the planet it orbits, our moon is the largest in the solar system. The moon partially helps protect the Earth from incoming mobile celestial beings such as asteroids.

The moon has a gravitational pull on Earth. This gravitational pull does several things. The Moon's gravitational force helps stabilize the tilt of the Earth, which is maintained at approximately 23.5°. This tilt assures us our seasons and assures our seasons are mild. The moon's orbit fluctuates by only 3.82 centimeters (1.5 inches) a year! No moon and our tilt would be much larger, creating poles with wildly fluctuating seasons. This would create a situation where no life would have the chance to have normal life cycles. The moon also helps regulate the Earth's spin. No moon and we would spin uncontrollably fast and if the moon were any larger we would slow our spin too much, and reduce our tilt resulting in a situation similar to Mars where one side of the plant is scorching hot and the other is a cozy, consistent -80° F (-62° C). Thus, the moon even helps our climate's unique maintenance.

Another major function of the moon is to increase our tides. Now, if you were anything like me, you would have trouble fathoming why tides would matter for life as we know it? The moon is responsible for sixty percent of our tidal power, the Sun, the other forty percent. As the tides goes out, it pulls with it nutrient minerals from the land into circulation in the ocean. These nutrients are consumed by microorganisms (tiny animals), some of which help maintain the O_2 (oxygen) and CO_2 (carbon dioxide) balance of our climate. Larger organisms consume these minerals as well, then larger organisms consume them and so on. Even the Great Blue Whale, the largest animal by mass to have ever lived on Earth, lives on tiny plankton and krill that feed on these mineral nutrients.

Circulating the ocean's water is important to assure the ocean's salt concentration does not get too high. Yes, you need water for life, but in a pure water world the salt concentration would first go extremely high, far too high even for halophiles (salt loving organisms). Without land the salt and all the minerals would just sink to the bottom, unusable. We would have this landless planet if our moon was any larger or if Earth was any larger. The reason for the latter being, the bigger the planet, the greater the surface gravity. If you increased Earth's size the surface gravity would flatten all the land and mountains. There is a tremendous amount of water within the Earth's crust, hence why you find drinking water when we drill into the Earth's crust. This water would be pushed out of the crust and the all the land would be under 6,562 feet (10,560 km) of water. One way that the moon helps regulate oceanic salt concentration is when the tide comes in the shallows, or shoals, the Sun heats the water and salt is deposited on the land. The tide then goes out and the salt is given back to the land.

Gravity is a crucial factor for balancing the forces of our universe. Gravity's particles, called gravitons, and no that is not a robot that can turn into a car, are relatively weak. We are only held down to Earth due to the gravity's collective effect on Earth's 6,000,000,000,000,000,000,000,000 (twenty one zeros) tons of matter. Gravity is also crucial to our health and development. It is this force that makes space medicine so difficult. Getting to Mars physically may be the relatively easy part but how do we compensate the toll of such little gravity on the human body. Astronauts lose a considerable amount of muscle and bone. The heart and lungs function differently as well. Thus, gravity even helps us on a physiological basis.

Unlike gravity, no other force can affect *everything* in the universe. Gravity exists on a space and time continuum. Gravity is the stage that the other forces of nature play on. Interesting, what else, if true, would affect everything and would exist in space and time? Albert Einstein is the only person who has gotten even close enough to explain the force of gravity via his general theory of relativity, but he, nor anyone else, has been able to explain the cause of gravity. No other force (electromagnetic or nuclear) has been described with such precision or over so many levels. General theory of relativity does a good job at calculating gravity but completely fails as it approaches quantum calculations, black holes, and the beginning of the universe, also known as the origin of the big bang.

In physics or mechanics, quantum denotes the minimum amount of any physical entity involved in an interaction. Another way to look at it is it describes the physical properties of nature on an atomic scale. Gravitational singularity is a region in spacetime where gravitational forces become infinite. The singularities of blackholes point to the location in space-time where it seems to become infinite and it is at this point the theory of relativity breaks down. Even if you incorporate quantum calculations to this area where very energetic gravitons are in play, you would have infinitely many infinite terms to calculate. One would have to add infinite number of counterterms in the equation in a never-ending process. Black holes can only be a consequence of gravity because gravity is the only force that is felt by *every* form of matter. If gravity were any other force of nature scientists could engineer technology capable of reaching ever greater energies and small distances, but gravity is no ordinary force. Other forces of nature are built on the theory of locality that states that the variables (things you must consider in an equation) describe what is going on at each point in space. Electromagnetic and nuclear force variables can change independently and their variable can only directly influence their immediate neighbors. Locality matters because it preserves causal (relating as a cause) relationship. In regard to the other forces scientists can remove entities of nature when making calculations that lead to sensible explanations and usually with a very high degree of accuracy. We cannot do this when it comes to quantum gravity.

In quantum gravity, space-time itself behaves in entirely unique ways. Unlike other forces of nature where we get creation of particles, gravity creates universes. In particles physics, fields of nature are superimposed on one another and extend into space. Space being one huge vacuum. That is why a hole in a spaceship, while in space, results in everything inside being sucked out into space (the vacuum), and I mean everything, objects as well as every molecule of oxygen. When considering gravity, we find that the expansion of the universe appears to produce more of this vacuum out of *nothing*. Gravity creates something from nothing! Sound familiar? When space-time is created, it just happens to be in the state that corresponds to the vacuum but without defects. No defects you say? How the vacuum appears precisely in the right arrangement is one of the main questions' physicists are attempting to answer in an effort to obtain a consistent quantum description of black holes and the origins of the universe. And yet, gravity is what holds everything together, perfectly. The best hypothesis to date is 'string theory' that states miniscule vibrating strings are what make up gravity. Vibrating strings? Strings of what? And who placed them there? How do they work?

Speaking of large matter and gravitational pull, let us consider Jupiter. Jupiter is also in an almost perfect spot in our solar system. Jupiter is so massive, yet at just the right distance to aid the Earth. For one, its massive size, and thus its gravity, help our orbit maintain an almost perfect circle. This keeps us at a consistent distance from the Sun and this gives Earth its consistent atmosphere and temperature. If Earth's orbit was more of an elliptical (oval) shape, then as the Earth reached the polar ends of the oval the Earth would freeze completely over. And then as the Earth reached the portion closest to the Sun, the Earth would reach scorching temperatures. Temperatures that would destroy all plant life, overheat the oceans, and make oxygen levels skyrocket. Hyperoxemia (too much oxygen in our blood) could occur, that is if the radiation did not kill us first. Hyperoxemia? But we breathe oxygen … yes, but we breathe just the right amount. At sea level the percentage of oxygen in our atmosphere is twenty one percent. As this percentage gets higher and higher our blood pressure would rise, nausea and vomiting would occur, along with tunnel vision, and ringing in the ears. Eventually random seizures would occur and eventually, death.

Jupiter is also a shield for our planet. With its mass and thus, powerful gravitational pull, it shields us from comets and space debris that may have the potential to strike Earth. Even Saturn and Uranus help with this too. Mars and our Moon are of tremendous help in shielding us from incoming asteroids. The asteroid belt is located between Jupiter and Mars. The planet named after the Roman god of war literally helps shield us. If you observe the surface of Mars and the moon, they are extensively covered with pot marks from asteroid and comet impacts.

Two

Earth Emblazoned

As stated earlier, the Earth is just the right size for the abundancy of life. Coupled with the perfectly sized and powerful Sun, as well as the size and location of the Moon, the statistical odds of all of this being chance begin to approach absurdity. The statistics of which will be discussed soon. To have a planet suitable for life you must have the right atmosphere. According to the current scientific literature, the Earth's atmosphere has changed tremendously over its 4.5 billion years. Sidebar: The Sun is 4.6 billion years old … that is an extremely short time period of difference between that and of the Earth, especially on the galactic timeline, this is 0.7 percent of the 14-billion-year-old universe. Back to the primary bar: The change in Earth's atmosphere has consisted of extreme levels of ammonia and methane that resulted in sweltering temperatures. These high temperatures and ultraviolet radiation resulted in water vaper being produced. The water vapor gave off oxygen (O_2), meanwhile volcanic eruptions and tectonic plate movements thrusted CO_2 (carbon dioxide) into the atmosphere. As the methane and ammonia levels decreased, the Earth cooled, and the high CO_2 levels resulted in gigantic plants and abundant floral growth. Around 4 billion years ago, bacteria emerged as the first non-flora living creatures.

The tectonic plates are important for maintaining life on Earth. Also, Earth is the only planet in our solar system that has tectonic plates. The tectonic plates move due to the heat generated by the radioactive isotopes. Wait, what is an isotope? An isotope is a molecule or element that is the same element but with a different number of neutrons in its nucleus (center). The plate tectonics drive minerals, CO_2, and O_2 into the mantle of the Earth. The mantle is the second layer of the Earth. You have the crust, which is what we live on, then the mantle, then the core. The mantle is filled with liquified minerals, mostly iron. The combustion of the gas and minerals within the mantle escape and are ventilated via volcanoes. This helps our planet regulate CO_2 levels, which is roughly 0.04 percent of Earth's atmosphere. Not to mention the 2.4 gigatons, or 5,291,094,292,437 pounds of CO_2 the oceans help buffer every year. Carbon dioxide is important for our atmosphere, in the correct amount. It is used to grow plants, absorb infrared radiation and by doing the latter it helps keep our planet warm.

The burning convection of the mantle keeps the iron within it liquid. It is this iron that generates the Earth's magnetic field! Our magnetic field shields us from cosmic rays and solar flares. With no magnetic field Earth would be flooded with high levels of radiation, resulting in scorching all living things and evaporating all the surface water. If the iron were cooler it would move slower, the iron would sink to the core and no magnetic field would exist. If there was more radioactivity, as there was during Earth's birth, the excessive volcanic ash would blot out the sun, and thus, like the newly formed Earth, no life would exist. Electric fields are generated around particles that bear electric charge. A moving charge always has both a magnetic and electric field, and that is precisely the reason why they are associated with each other. The electrical field of the Earth out pulls the gravitational force by a factor of 10^{39}! Just how big is that? Stack 10^{39} atoms end to end, and it would reach the end of the universe and back 1,000 times.

An atmosphere is also necessary to protect the planets life from overwhelming ultraviolet radiation. The majority of our atmosphere is nitrogen ($\approx$ seventy-eight percent). Nitrogen is the most significantly important element for fertilizing our plants. It also just happens to be inert within our lungs. Meaning the nitrogen does no harm to our lungs. Why not sulfur? Or phosphorus? Or fluoride? Or carbon dioxide? Or helium? Or argon? No, it is nitrogen, which again, is neutral in our lungs and the best element for helping the plants to grow. Plants grow and breathing organisms receive the oxygen they give off during photosynthesis (using light for energy creation). But back to the developing atmosphere of the Earth.

Slowly oxygen levels began to climb and then, for reasons unknown to science, the oxygen content of the atmosphere increased exponentially. This occurred approximately 541 million years ago which corresponds with an era known as the Cambrian explosion. The fossils found from the Cambrian explosion is marked by the appearance of many anatomical body types, as if out of nowhere, but we will cover this in unit two. Okay, one more fun fact, our friends the dinosaurs, first appeared around 247 million years ago. Sorry, I had to sneak that fact in now after I said we'd talk about it later just because dinosaurs are so cool! Thus, the new oxygen rich atmosphere fostered the incredible expansion of life on Earth.

Carbon dioxide, magnetic fields, and ozone (O_3) are all working to keep our radiation levels down, but it is still not quite enough to permit life as we know it to exist. Albedo is another effect that helps the planet reflect sunlight. Yes, albedo, not libido. Albedo refers to the proportion of sunlight a planet reflects. Earth has several albedo factors. The oceans, polar ice caps, deserts, and snow are all involved in reflecting the Sun's light off the Earth's surface. This is one of the reasons we can sunburn under our chin when we play in the snow. No albedo and the Earth would be blanketed in so much radiation life could not exist. Everything has its place and purpose. The entire continental portion of the United States can fit within the boundaries of the Sahara Desert of Africa, the second largest desert on Earth. The largest desert being Antarctica. Yeah, didn't know deserts were so important, did ya? So, now we take all the ingredients discussed in chapters one and two, which were just a few of the thirty or so components necessary to create a planet suitable for life, and we discover that all we needed was the right sized Sun, moon, planet, protective planets (Jupiter, Mars), have tectonic plates, liquid iron core, be in the safe zone of the galaxy, water, the most appropriate elements of the 118 known elements, the right number of atoms, albedo, and just the right amount of gravity and boom, you are ready to inhabit life.

Not accounting for the statistical odds of life forming, just purely the odds of the rock we call Earth forming to be suitable for life is one in 700,000,000,000,000,000,000 (700 quintillion). Your odds of winning the Powerball® is roughly one in 175,000,000. Coincidences and impossible randomness, is that how we want to settle the dispute of our universe's formation and development?

PART II

LIVELY LIFE

Three

BASIC BIO

Biology is the study of life. Life is defined as any organism that has the capacity for growth, reproduction, and functional activity. For the most part this book will focus on human biology, but many of the same biological functions occur in other species. As mentioned in part one, atoms are the smallest particles that exist and is what everything is made of. Two or more atoms joining together is a molecule. It is in the molecular form that the vast majority of chemical reactions and functions take place. Atoms stick together via their electron clouds. To put it simply, they share electrons. For example, Na^+ is a single atom of sodium, Cl^- is a single atom of chloride, and $NaCl$ together makes a molecule, called sodium chloride, also known as table salt. A 154.3-pound (seventy kg) human consists of approximately 7,000,000,000,000,000,000,0 00,000,000 atoms and over 1,000,000,000 cells (phew). There are estimated to be 10^{79} (seventy-nine zeros!) of atoms in the entire universe. There are approximately 1,000,000,000,000 (1 trillion) atoms in the average animal cell. To make a human you need at least twenty-six essential elements, although up to sixty have been identified in the human body. Bacteria require at least sixteen essential elements. It is thus important to remember that just having H_2O (water) on the planet does not necessarily mean life can exist. As a matter of fact, while making a protein, water needs to be removed in order for each amino acid to be joined together. Additionally, the presence of water strongly inhibits amino acids from forming proteins. Amino acids will actually dissolve in water. You need perfect balance. Scientists thus must describe a scenario where life or protein origin develop without being within water itself (e.g. primordial slime). But I thought water was crucial for developing life? It is, but in the right place and with other correct biological sequences.

Biochemistry is the study of chemicals and their functions within a living system. Physiology and molecular biology are related fields. For the purposes of this book they will all be lumped together. When scientists research and discuss these topics, it is many times done at the cellular level. The cell is the smallest structural and functional unit of an organism. Some species only need one cell to exist (e.g. bacteria). Cells are microscopic and there are roughly 200 different cell types. You have cells unique and specific to the heart, for the liver, for the skin, and so on. Within the cells there are its functioning parts, called organelles. I always remember by recalling that the human body has organs and the little cell has its own organs called organelles. The most famous organelle is the nucleus. This is the housing unit for the deoxyribonucleic acid, also known as DNA; the famous double-helix shaped complex molecule that resembles the twist-tie at the end of a bread bag (see graph 3). Every animal species on Earth houses its genetic material on DNA within a nucleus. Some viruses have just ribonucleic acid (RNA) for their genetic material, however, viruses are not technically living things, but I digress.

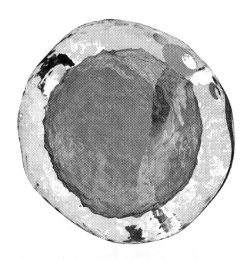

*[**Graph 2**: The nucleus is the darker spherical image in the center of the cell. The nucleus contains the double stranded DNA within it.]*

DNA is the coding system for the production of proteins. Proteins are the molecules that carry out most of the functions of the organism's body. If the protein carries out a biochemical conversion function or process, we call it an enzyme. I picture enzymes as the labor force of the protein class. The chemical reactions of the cell would not occur rapidly enough to sustain life if enzymes were not present. Enzymes are usually highly specific for their substrates (the substance acted upon) and products. A complete set of genes present in a cell or organism is called a genome. The genome is carried on structures known as chromosomes. Some chromosomes are for phenotypic expression. Pheno what? This is just a fancy word for genes that are expressed in a visual fashion. A person's facial structure, hair color, and eye color are phenotypic expressions. We are visually attracted to another person's phenotype (wink). Whereas a genotype is a fancy term for genes that are unseen, such as our immune system, cardiac (heart) system, and other more internal workings. The DNA uses four biochemicals called nucleic acids in order to communicate their information. Easy to remember since it shares the prefix nucle-. Phew!

Similar to that of the binary system of computers this is a quaternary system (system of four components) that combine with each other to create a code for the roughly 30,000 proteins of the human body. Proteins are made of amino acids, which we will get into greater detail later. The deoxyribonucleic acid (DNA) structure; is the double helix. This structure must be unwound, one side of it copied to make a *single* helix strip of messenger ribonucleic acid (mRNA) that leaves the nucleus to a protein called ribosome. The ribosome "reads" the mRNA and helps attach amino acid to amino acid in order to make a protein.

The newborn protein is not complete yet, it then must go to an organelle called the endoplasmic reticulum to be folded and prepared for departure. Wait, so you finally tell us how a protein is made, and we have more to go? Yes. We have the statistically improbable task of even creating a protein with the complex DNA, nucleus, and protein apparatus, and now you tell me the protein is not even complete? Yes. The protein being incomplete also means it is not functional yet. The immature protein then travels from the endoplasmic reticulum to the golgi apparatus for the final stage of completion. The final protein is bundled into a vesicle, which is like a cellular membrane within the cellular membrane, or small sac. When the protein is complete or needed, this vesicle is formed and leaves the golgi apparatus and travels to the cellular membrane where it fuses with the membrane and spits out (exocytosis) the proteins for the body to use (see graph 4). The process of protein finalization literally requires 100 pages in a textbook to explain, you are welcome. Of course, many proteins are used within the cell to conduct cellular function. The cell even has a skeleton! It is primarily made of a protein called *actin* and this gives the cell structures but also creates a highway some other proteins use to travel upon. Picture rebar, the steel mesh used within concrete to reinforce the concrete and give it structure. In the same way, the skeleton of the cell, called the cytoskeleton, reinforces the cell and gives it structural support.

Summary: DNA is that famous double helix we all know so well (see Graph 3). The four bases of nucleic acids are paired together, and we call them base pairs. Each human cell has billions and billions of base pairs. These base pairs must code perfectly to make RNA. Picture RNA as the messenger for the DNA. The double helix of DNA is unwound at just the right spot, then cut in just the right spot, and then copied in order to make the messenger RNA that takes the template to the ribosomes waiting outside of the nucleus. Amino acids are the building blocks of protein. Picture them as the individual bricks in a Lego® playset. These bricks are organized in a specific pattern in order to form a protein and this is dictated by the code on the messenger RNA. The ribosome has the mRNA run through it like a ribbon through a wringer and amino acids are added to the developing protein based on that mRNA's code. The protein is then reshaped for functional preparation and voilà, a baby protein is born.

DNA replication

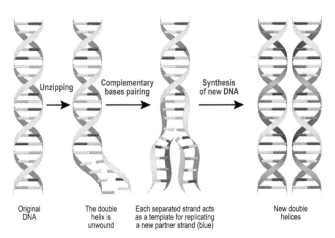

Unzipping   Complementary   Synthesis
bases pairing   of new DNA

| Original DNA | The double helix is unwound | Each separated strand acts as a template for replicating a new partner strand (blue) | New double helices |

*[**Graph 3**: The deoxyribonucleic acid (DNA) structure; the double helix. This structure must be unwound, one side of it copied to make a single helix strip of messenger ribonucleic acid (mRNA) which then leaves the nucleus to a protein called ribosome which reads the mRNA and helps attach amino acid to amino acid in order to make a protein.]*

ENDOPLASMIC RETICULUM AND GOLGI APPARATUS
PROTEIN SYNTHESIS AND DISTRIBUTION

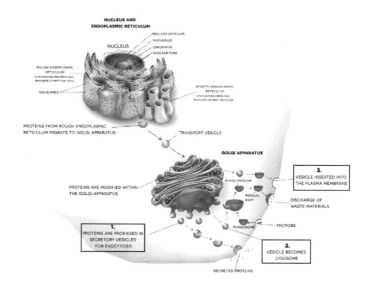

*[**Graph 4**: The organelles involved in the making of a protein.]*

The cell cannot exist with just its organelles, it needs a protective container. Thus, the cell has a wall called the cellular membrane. It is a phospholipid bilayer; lipid means fat like. Picture what happens when you pour olive oil into water or a vinaigrette. Notice how the oil, which is fat, consolidates to itself and does not mix with the solution it was placed into? This is similar to how our cells maintain a wall or barrier that keeps the contents inside and the environment out. Now this cellular membrane is more complex than that. It contains cholesterol that strengthens the barrier and dozens of proteins (fifty percent of the cell membrane). The cell membrane proteins communicate with passing hormones, proteins, and other cells. There are also some specialized sugars (carbohydrates) in the membrane, they help bind cells together and facilitate cell to cell recognition so that they know when to stop growing during reproduction or repair. What is even more incredible is the cell membrane cannot just form by itself. Meaning there is a cellular production for the membrane and if there was no membrane there would be no life. Many amateur scientists believe all you need is some amino acids, nucleic acids, and water and nature will figure out the rest. Wrong!

So, why did I tell you all of this? I thought this book was supposed to be written for the non-scientist. Yes, it most certainly is, but in order to appreciate the complexity of cellular function we need to explain the foundation of biology. I would also recommend book marking this portion of the text and use it as a reference.

Before Life

According to current scientific dogma all we need is some amino acids, nucleic acids, water, and lightening and poof, you have life. This is like equating learning to count to three to learning quantum physics equations with imaginary numbers. Even a basic amino acid like glycine has two carbon atoms, two oxygen atoms, five hydrogen atoms, and one nitrogen atom, and all of that must come together perfectly in order to be functional. They also cannot just simply link together, they need messenger RNA, the protein ribosome, and transfer RNA. Oh, and you need the DNA that originally coded for all these proteins, including the ribosome (what came first, the DNA or the ribosome?) You also need a safe and constant environment for all of them to function in, like a cellular membrane and nucleus. The greatest statistical odd is then getting not only the amino acids all together but then fold the protein into the correct shape, and then it must be functional! The statistical odds of even a simple protein (low amino acid count) randomly going from its primary form (like a string of pearls) to its final form (globular structure like bubbles in a bubble bath) are one in 10^{125th} or one with 125 zeros behind it! In the world of mathematics this is essentially a zero percent chance.

That astronomical figure is for a simple protein. There are approximately 30,000 proteins in the human body. One of the smallest known proteins is *villin*, which is thirty-five amino acids in size. The largest known human protein is *titin* which is 34,350 amino acids in size. There are twenty amino acids in total, including well known ones like alanine and tryptophan. And remember, even single celled organisms such as bacteria require roughly 265 – 350 different proteins to sustain life. As humans, as well as other complex animals, we not only have DNA to produce the proteins necessary for life and complex existence, but we also have cells that contain DNA that can learn new codes in order to make new protein. A great example of this is our immune system. Our immune system can learn about new invaders and produce a protein called an antibody that is specific to that unique invader and if the invader tries to get into our bodies again the immune system is able to dispose of it quickly.

Amino acids all have a couple things in common, they require nitrogen and carbon. Carbon is an incredible atom because it has the ability to bind with up to four other atoms. This makes it great for creating complex structures necessary for life. The Earth is thought to be 4.5 billion years old with life showing up a mere 500 million years later. The first life forms were single celled organisms, i.e. bacteria. Due to the fact that plants and proteins require nitrogen you would expect the Earth's crust strata (layers) of that time period to contain extensive amounts of nitrogen, correct? Nope, strata from that era was found to only have 0.15 percent nitrogen, and even though Earth formed 4.5 billion years ago, the climate was far too harsh for life, so life had to wait for the cool down period, as well as the right atmospheric conditions. The latter dependent on the former. This then narrowed the time frame life had to emerge to *100 million years*. Keep this number in mind when we discuss the statistical odds of even just proteins and other life compounds forming.

Once we had single celled organisms a couple other very basic organisms sprout up and nothing changes for almost 3.5 billion years, then, all of a sudden, oxygen levels sky rocket, and the fossils found in the strata of the Earth revealed twenty to thirty-five different body types, with no predecessors! There are currently forty. We went from no limb to limbs, no intestinal tract to complex ones; no vertebrae (spinal cord) to vertebrae. If life was supposed to evolve in a systematic sequence from single cell, to let's say a worm like creature, to perhaps a fish, to then a two legged animal, to a four legged animal there should be clear evidence of this transition in the fossil record, but it does not exist. This momentous event occurred roughly 541 million years ago and is known as the Cambrian explosion. Forget the 'missing link' we are missing all the links!

Four

THE CHICKEN OR THE EGG

Genes and Proteins

Before I discuss the intricacies of genes and the proteins they produce, I would like to give you some probability solutions mathematicians have deciphered given the known entities of biology. The odds of the random evolution of a *single*, 150 amino acid, is one in $10^{164\text{th}}$. Remember our friend the protein ribosome? It is a 300 amino acid protein and its chances of random formation to functional form is four to $10^{180\text{th}}$. Now, have some fun and imagine the statistical odds of the 34,350 amino acid sized protein *titin*. These odds are the same as blind folding yourself, and having you solve a Rubix® cube, oh and you have to make one move per second. This would take you 1.35 trillion years to complete. The odds against each move producing a color match are $5^{10,000,000,000,000,000,000}$ to 1. The odds of the approximately 2,000 enzymes (action proteins) randomly forming are the same as rolling a dice and achieving 50,000 sixes perfectly in a row. So, life showed up 4 billion years ago, yet the odds of a single, 150 amino acid protein randomly evolving would take 1.35 trillion years? This is ninety-six times the proposed age of the universe, let alone life on Earth.

A single celled organism, such as the bacterium *Escherichia coli's* (E. coli's), chance of randomly arising in the prebiotic soup, during the proposed timeline it had to develop, is one in $10^{1100\text{th}}$. That is

1,100 zeros. A trillion has only twelve zeros. If you were to show a mathematician these types of numbers, they would laugh at the number and then tell you to just say zero, because for all intents and purposes this statistic is equal to zero. Even Carl Sagan, famed physicist, and self-admitted atheist, estimated the percentile chance of human evolution to be $10^{-2,000,000,000}$ percent ... that negative sign indicates all those zeros are *after* the decimal point. Again, write out 2,000,000,000 zeros after a decimal point and put the number one at the end of it. This is an unfathomable number. Truly, the human mind cannot comprehend such a figure. Again, in many math classes this number could be marked zero and you would be correct.

Each cell contains six feet of DNA. DNA by itself, can do nothing. It requires proteins to unwind it, copy it, reproduce it, and maintain it. Proteins are made from the written directions of the DNA, so which came first? There are also proteins that help correct mistakes that are made during the replication of genetic material. This incredibly complex process also requires energy. Thus, an energy producing apparatus had to evolve simultaneously. So, let us start from the beginning, and even this explanation will be elementary.

First a protein called *helicase* (hel-eh-caze) unwinds the DNA's double helix structure. Easy to remember because of the prefix heli-. Proteins that end in -ase are the enzymes. How does it know where to attach among the billions of base pairs? The short answer is we do not know. In *E. coli* a protein called *dnaA* attaches to the DNA and is the spot where the helicase attaches to. While this is occurring, a protein called *DNA gyrase* (ji-raze) moves ahead of the helicase in order to relieve torsional stress of the DNA. Picture the DNA gyrase as a loosening the double helix in order to make the helicase's job easier.

The goal here is to replicate a strip of this DNA into a single strip of genetic material, RNA (ribonucleic acid). This ribbon strip of RNA carries just the 'codes' needed to make a specific protein. A protein called *RNA polymerase* (pah-leh-mer-aze) is the protein that is responsible for copying this cleaved portion of the DNA strand. Once the specific segment is complete the protein *RNA hydrolase* (hi-dro-laze) cuts the completed RNA strip from the DNA. Now the DNA has to be patched back together into that lovely double helix shape. This is accomplished by *DNA polymerase α* (alpha) replacing the nucleotides and *DNA ligase* (lie-gaze) reattaching the DNA segments to the other side of the double helix. There is even a special enzyme called *telomerase* (te-lo-mer-aze) that helps prevent the loss of genetic material. Question for you, before evolution accomplished its ultimate goal of creating life, what happened after DNA gyrase did its job but there was no RNA polymerase yet?

So now we have this strip of RNA, what are we to do with it? This strip of RNA is now called messenger RNA or mRNA, leaves the nucleus of the cell, and enters the cytoplasm, or open space of the cell. The mRNA will attach to a ribosome, the ribbon strip of mRNA runs through it, and within every three sets of nucleotide code there is an amino acid that corresponds to it. The code is decoded by another set of RNA called transfer RNA or tRNA, and this carries the appropriate amino acid for that set of nucleotide base pairs. The next three nucleotides come through and attach to the previous amino acid and so on and so on (see graph 5). Eventually you have a brand new, yet non-functional protein or peptide chain (peptide, yet another term for protein). The completion of the functional protein was discussed in chapter three.

RIBOSOME

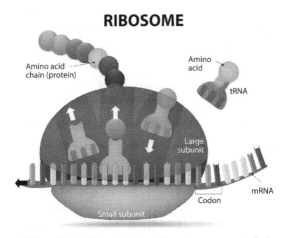

[**Graph 5**: *The making of a primary peptide.*]

All in all, there are dozens of proteins involved in DNA replication and over fifty proteins involved in RNA processing alone. Like a machine in a factory production line, a mistake can occur at any point of the process. If the endoplasmic reticulum does not trim up the protein in just the right way, or if the Golgi apparatus does not fold the protein in to it's perfect shape, then even though the DNA and RNA did their job well, the protein is non-functional. Let us reflect on that from an evolutionary standpoint; we already discussed the problem of what came first, the DNA or protein? If we are left with a formed protein but it is not cut, folded, and correctly packaged, it still will do absolutely nothing for the organism. The odds are not looking favorable.

What if a mistake occurs during DNA or RNA production? Well they do and at a rate of roughly one in every 1,000,000,000 nucleotides copied. The primary argument of macroevolution is that minute changes of DNA occur to improve the survival chances of the organism and their species. This problem is two-fold, for one, the fossil record shows no evidence for this, and second, almost all mutations that occur in the DNA is detrimental to the organism. A good example of this is cancer. Cancer results from multiple mutations in the DNA, this then produces a cell that does not know when to stop growing. When a person has a deformity or is lacking a crucial protein we say, oh, it is a genetic disorder. Again, implying the changes in DNA were detrimental. A classic example of good genetic intentions gone bad is sickle cell disease. Sickle cell anemia is a disease of which our red blood cells, the cells responsible for carrying oxygen from our lungs to our body, are mishappened and look like a sickle under a microscope. I would have used the word crescent, for crescent moon shaped, but I was not in charge of that decision-making process. Scientists believe this occurred as a result of the body's attempt to combat malaria, a blood parasite that lives inside the red blood cells of its host. This hypothesis was made because those who suffer with the affliction are those people indigenous to the equatorial regions where malaria flourishes and the sickle shape seems to have some protective qualities against malaria. Notice I said suffer with; because although this may seem to help with malaria it renders the red blood cell ineffective. This results in damage to the host and in most cases ends in death.

Since trillions of genetic replications are occurring in our bodies at any one time, it is safe to say there are many mistakes being made and yet we do not suffer. This is because the body does a great job of catching the mistakes and correcting them. If you review graph two you will see the four nucleotides there, adenine, guanine, cytosine, and thymine. There is a fifth one called uracil, but this only used in RNA. Adenine should always pair with thymine and cytosine should always pair with guanine. A to T and G to C! Sickle cell anemia results from just a single base change! This is called a point mutation because a single base pair has changed. Some DNA polymerase enzymes exhibit 'proofreading' qualities and can catch mistakes before they get past the replication phase. When the sun damages DNA's helical shape there is actually a protein called *DNA photolyase* that can remove the damaged portion. If it were not for this, many of us would have skin cancer (melanoma) by our twenties. Since humans have two complementary strands of DNA, one of them can be used as a template should the other strand have a defect.

A mismatch occurs when instead of an A to T match or a G to C, an A to C or T to G occurs. When this occurs, there is a protein made up of multiple proteins that scan the DNA for a mistake. When one is found, an enzyme called *endonuclease* (endo means inside and nucleo- means nucleus) cleaves the strand closest to the mistake. The enzyme *DNA polymerase III* copies from the complementary strand of DNA and the newly produced segment is put in place of the old one by *DNA ligase.*

A base-excision repair helps in situations where the DNA has been incorrectly processed chemically. This process involves cutting out a specific base; this is achieved by a group of enzymes called *glycosylase* (gly-kah-sil-aze). Two more enzymes then prep the site and an enzyme called *DNA polymerase I* inserts the appropriate nucleotide base into the space and *DNA ligase* seals it in place. And there you have it, like it never even happened.

A third way that our cells repair point mutations is via a nucleotide excision. This simply means the erroneous nucleotide is cut out. This process involves multiple enzymes in humans and other non-bacteria organisms. Here an entire nucleotide pair is removed and replaced. A defect in this form of repair, seen in such cases involving *DNA photolyase* can result in a disease called xeroderma pigmentosa. In this disease there is a decreased ability to repair sun (UV) damaged DNA. This results in sun burning when just in the sun for a few minutes, dry skin, and early life melanoma. Xero- means dry, derma- means skin, and pigment refers to cells that can produce pigmentation (skin color).

Scientists have named certain segments of the genome typically when we, a) know what it codes for, or b) we know what happens when a disease occurs there. The enzymes previously mentioned in DNA and RNA biological happenings have their own portions of the genome with codes just for their production. For example, *DNA helicase* is located on the ATRX gene, *RNA polymerase* is on the POLR2A gene, and *DNA ligase* is on the LIG1 gene, and so on. If just one of these proteins are missing genetic replication and reproduction cease. In biology we call this 'irreducible complexity.' This means that the system is already at its most reduced state in order to function and by removing just one aspect of it the system fails to function, or at minimum, function properly. Thousands of biochemical processes fall into this category. There are some diseases that result in a partially functioning protein, and although the organism may live, the living is not exactly pleasant. Again, I will ask, if you need these genes to produce these proteins, but you need proteins to reproduce the genetic material ... which came first?

Let us say a genetic change occurs, it cannot just be passed on to future generations just like that. The change must be displayed on the genetic code within the gametes. Gametes are the reproductive cells of males and females, sperm, and ova respectively. If the mutations are not encoded into these cells, then no future generation will display that genetic change. And even if the change does get there, and it is only present in one parent, it still may not be expressed in the offspring. Oh, and to make matters worse, the gamete cells are 1,000 times less likely to have a mutation compared to all the other cells of the body.

Five

THE OBEISANT BODY

Growing a Human

"In the absence of any other proof, the thumb alone would convince me of God's existence." – Sir Isaac Newton.

Embryogenesis is the field of science dedicated to learning about how life develops as a result of reproduction. This may be a biased opinion based on the fact that embryogenesis fascinates me to no end, but I would wager the development of a fetus is the single most complex process in the entire known universe. There is a reason everyone says, "the miracle of birth." As stated previously, the cellular processes of bacteria are far more complicated than the physics of the stars and planets. And thusly, in the world of biology, embryogenesis is the most intricate.

Fertilization alone is on a complexity that rivals the creation of the universe and it could fill thousands of pages of textbooks to explain its intricacies. Simply contemplating the mere splicing of the genetic material from a sperm and ovum (egg) is enough to give one a headache musing. When a fetus is developing, not only do the developing cells have to do all of the ordinary functions of a cell, they must also differentiate into all of the different tissue types and assure those types end up in the correct place. How do they know where to go? How do they avoid becoming entangled with all the arteries, veins, nerves, and lymphatic vessels? The short answer is transcription factors. These are specialized gene proteins that control the rate of transcription (copying) of genetic information from DNA to messenger RNA. Transcription factors can turn on and off genes in order to make sure they are expressed in the right cells at the right time. There are an estimated 1,600 known transcription factors in the human genome. They work in the adult body as well, but their most daunting challenge and most important task is regulating embryogenesis.

We will now go through all 1,600 transcription factors. Number one … just kidding. Dictating the direction of growth and placement of limbs and organs is one of the most crucial jobs of transcription factors. They must assure that the liver ends up in the abdomen and the brain ends up inside the neurocranium (skull). Limb development is regulated by the transcription factor group Hox. For example, Hox9D with HoxD10, Fgf4, and BMP4 help develop the humeral region, which is your arm. Hox is expressed in multiple organisms, even snakes, which have no limbs. Scientists propose that as evolution progressed limbless creatures of the ocean emerged on land and developed limbs. After a while, the organisms destined to become snakes turned off their Hox genes. HoxC6 is present in snakes to *suppress* forelimb formation. Scientists report that the regulatory switches were harnessed during the acquisition of limbs through evolution and then they were turned off during the evolution of limbless species. Thus, snakes lost their forearms to evolution by evolving a gene to suppress the development of their forelimbs … does that make sense to you? And although the snake does a great job at what it does, does this finding indicate being limbless is evolutionarily superior to developing limbs?

The Notch signaling pathway is involved in determining cell fate, particularly in regard to blood vessels and nerves. Blood is required for any cellular growth because it supplies the tissues with oxygen and nutrients. The development of arteries takes a certain amount of precedence in the hierarchy of development. Because it is so important for blood to reach all portions of the developing fetus it must have overriding powers in order to tell other developing tissue to get out of its way. Arteries develop under the influence of the transcription factor Efnb2. Nerves are the next important structure to end up in the precise locations it needs to be. Nerves sense the world around us and provide the signal for our muscles to contract. Interestingly many of our primary arteries and nerves are anatomically very close to one other. The opposite is true in regard to veins and lymphatic tissue. Veins drain the blood that has just finished delivering nutrients and oxygen to the distal tissue and return it to the heart and lungs so the blood can pick up more oxygen and be sent back out to the periphery. Lymphatic tissue develops from veins that did not quite finish their venous development, but are still crucial for draining fluid from tissue, as well as play a pivotal role in our immune system. During embryogenesis, arteries and nerves use transcription factors to tell veins and lymphatics to get out of their way. We call these transcription factors repulsion molecules and one of the key ones discovered for blood vessels is Netrin. Netrin signals through UNC5 receptors to coordinate with vascular endothelial growth factor-A (VEGF-A) from blood vessels to assure they avoid one another. As its name hints at, vascular endothelial growth factor stimulates the growth of arteries. Netrin is there though to play offense line and clear a path for the artery to grow. In nerve tissue Semaphorin 3 (Sema3) acts as repulsive molecules in axonal guidance and nerve cell migration. The axon is the long thread of tissue we classically associate when we picture a nerve. The place that the axon sprouts from is the nerve cell itself, where its nucleus is housed (see graph 6).

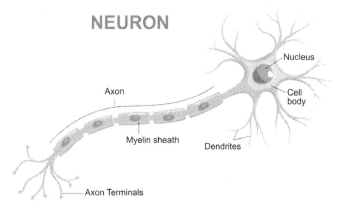

NEURON

Nucleus

Axon

Cell body

Myelin sheath

Dendrites

Axon Terminals

*[**Graph 6**: The anatomy of a nerve.]*

How does this tissue avoid running into developing connective tissue such as bone? Or not wrap around it? Many nerves and arteries have to actually pass through channels and holes in bone. Most of this is achieved through the interplay of the transcription factors bone morphogenic protein (BMP) and neural transcription factors such as Sema3. The greatest example of this interplay are the cranial nerves. The cranial nerves consist of twelve pairs of nerves that originate from the brain or brainstem, with only one exception. Since they originate centrally, these nerves must pass through portions of the skull in order to reach their target organ; whether this be our eyes, tongue, saliva producing glands, or the muscles we use to chew food with. For example, the 7th cranial nerve (CN VII) controls the muscles of facial expression, tear glands, and some salivary glands, and originates in the brainstem. It is accompanied by the 8th cranial nerve (CN VIII) which is responsible for hearing as well as helping us with head and neck balance. Together they travel through a canal deep in the skull, deep to our ears. They then split off with CN VIII heading to the hearing and balance organ of the ear and CN VII travels through yet another canal in the skull before dividing into dozens of branches to head to their respective target tissues.

The Brain

The human brain is what separates us from the other species of the planet and from the species we are most closely genetically related to, the primates, the advanced development of our frontal lobe is what separates us from them. The frontal lobe is the part of the brain just behind your forehead. It is also known as the neocortex (neo meaning new), which indicates this is the newest part of our brain, evolutionarily speaking. The frontal lobe is where our intellect resides, including forethought, and judgement. Complex emotions are housed here as well. Even though this is the newer portion of our brain there is still a connection to our emotional center, the limbic system. When Wolfgang Amadeus Mozart's Requiem brings a tear to your eye or reading a story of love increases your heart rate, or gives you goosebumps, it is your frontal lobe communicating with your limbic system.

The limbic system is present in many animals but ours is much larger and more complicated. Our frontal lobe allows us to ponder the universe and the meaning of life, as well as help a surgeon recall how to perform a surgery. Nerves communicate with brain chemicals called neurotransmitters (thank goodness, a word that makes a little sense). Our brains contain approximately 86,000,000,000 nerve cells (neurons) and 400 miles of blood vessels coursing through it. The eye grows and extends directly from the brain and converts light particles (photons) bouncing off objects into vision. The eye and its retina (the back portion of the eye) perform tasks every 1/3 of a second, which would take a supercomputer 100 years to do. Touch the very back of your skull (head); deep to that is the occipital lobe of the brain. This lobe is completely dedicated to vision. The brain can store 4,700,000,000 books worth of information and carry out 1,000,000,000,000,000 (1 quadrillion) logical operations a second. As of 2020, no supercomputer on Earth comes close to this capability.

Neurotransmitters are chemical signaling molecules that inform different parts of the nervous system what to do and what not to do. When we colloquially speak of neurotransmitters, we identify them incorrectly, such as dopamine being the 'happy' neurotransmitter or oxytocin being the 'love' hormone. This is not only false but minimizes the intricacy of these biochemical entities. When the scientist and neurosurgeon, Dr. Wilder Penfield, electrically probed the brain in an attempt to trigger different actions, and he could never cause the subject to believe something or make decisions. I would wager he also was never able to make the subject fall in love with something or someone. These more sophisticated emotions are unique to humans. Which neurotransmitter is responsible for the tearing induced by Mozart's Requiem or a rock ballad? What electrical signal is responsible for pondering the universe and all of its mysteries? The short answer is science does not know. Not that they will never know (although the discovery of this is unlikely because it is not necessarily physical), but for all of our incredible advancements in science the human brain is still the least understood organ of the entire body. You cannot label a part of the anatomy or label a neurotransmitter love, hate, sad, or happy; we are far more complex than this.

There is something unique and invisible about the human mind. Memories do have a physicality to them, but only to a certain extent. Memories are formed on proteins and stored in different regions of the temporal and frontal lobes. Humans have several types of memory: working, episodic, sensory, and procedural. Animals have memories as well but on a simpler, more survival-oriented manner. A deer may remember a meadow where it was once attacked by a cougar and thus be extra cautious when approaching that meadow. A chimpanzee may remember which area of the jungle has the best fruit; interestingly, they also have innate hydrophobia or fear of water, likely due to their high muscle density. I could write an entire book on all the deeper, more sophisticated memories and thoughts humans have over the other animals. Guilt, shame, moral and ethical decision making are complex human emotions. Our emotion of guilt after doing something we believe to be morally wrong is a uniquely human emotion. For instance, you never observe emotional suicide in animals based on how they feel about themselves. Yes, we see animals mourn for their lost companions such as in dogs and elephants but things like self-loathing, self-deprecation, and guilt are uniquely human. What gene controls that? What neurotransmitter is the self-loathing neurotransmitter?

Sending a signal down a nerve is a physical act and not sufficient to explain the complexities of our brain. What about our ability to do calculus or send a satellite into space? What neurotransmitter or gene allowed William Shakespeare to compose his masterpieces? How about music? Not only can we create music and build the instruments to play it, but we can have a deep emotional reaction to hearing it. No scientist knows the answer to these questions yet. However, we have mapped the human genome, analyzed molecules of the brain, and examined the anatomy of the brain under powerful microscopes, which makes the odds of us figuring this mystery out less and less likely.

Irreducible Protein Systems

Human blood is considered an organ and is filled with some of the most complex biological systems known to humankind. The average child has 60,000 miles of blood vessels and the average adult has nearly 100,000 miles of blood vessels. To put that in some perspective the circumference of the Earth is 24,901 miles. The heart beats 2,500,000,000 times in a lifetime. Each day the heart beats roughly 100,000 times and pumps 1,900 gallons (7,200 liters) of blood.

In chapter four we discussed the concept of irreducibly complex systems as it relates to biology. The clotting cascade of blood is another excellent example of an irreducibly complex system. The clotting cascade is a series of events involving ten or so proteins to accomplish the goal of stopping a bleed. Remove one protein and the bleeding does not stop. As a matter of fact, when pharmaceutical companies look to develop the latest blood thinner (anticoagulant) they look to which of these proteins is best to block from working. Oh, and many of these proteins are dependent on Vitamin K for production, a vitamin we consume but of which the bacteria in our gut are the primary producers. We humans then have another set of proteins involved in breaking down and disposing of the blood clot once it has accomplished its goal of stopping the bleed and sealing the wound long enough for the body to heal the injury. There are even regulator proteins of the clotting cascade and if they did not exist there would be unregulated clotting or bleeding. *Protein C* and *Protein S* are two of the primary regulators of the clotting cascade. These make sure, along with a few other proteins, that our blood clotting system does not get out of control. People with *Protein C* or *Protein S* deficiency can form clots anywhere and at any time and this is just from a deficiency. Not only does the protein have to be there, but there has to be a certain amount of it for their regulatory functions to operate completely. Once a clot has begun forming how does it know when or where to stop? Well, many proteins are involved but a protein called *antithrombin* attaches to the actively forming clot proteins and inactivates them. In the presence of the protein *heparin*, this task is carried out very rapidly. Another way that our body helps regulate the growing clot is *Protein C*. Protein C destroys the protein *accelerin* (speeds up the clotting process) and activates *antihemophilic factor*. Antihemophilic factor, as its name denotes, anti-blood-lover, helps assure the clot does not grow out of control. The first half of the theory of evolution is that random mutations occurred, followed by more specific mutations, but verily I say unto you, if any of the proteins involved in the clotting cascade, whether forming or dismantling the clot, were absent, nothing would regulate our bloods ability to clot or de-clot. Thus, our ancient ancestors either bled out constantly or died from forming clots in the blood stream, or, this biochemical system was engineered simultaneously and worked from day one.

Tissue plasminogen (plaz-min-o-jen) activator or tPA is one of the primary proteins involved in the breakdown of clots. There are four domains in the genetic code that house the information to make tPA and these four domains are spread out within 30,000 genes. The odds of getting those four domains together is $30,000^4$ to 1. If you had these kinds of odds while playing the lottery, and you took a million people playing, it would take 1,000,000,000,000 years before even one person won. Please remember we are talking about one protein out of 30,000+ proteins. This figure alone is eleven times longer than the estimated age of life on Earth. This number is actually conservative, because you would still need the four domains to be in the active area of the genome, have the correct splicing sequence, and of course the compatible amino acids, but I digress.

Intrinsic factor (IF) is a protein made in the stomach and is necessary for the absorption of vitamin B_{12} (cyanocobalamin). No *IF*, no B_{12}. No B_{12} and the result is anemia (low red blood cells), psychosis, and uncoordinated movement. I must ask the question, before we evolved to attain the *IF* protein, did our species just stumble around psychotic and then die from anemia? I am being sassy, but I hope you are beginning to see the point that this crucial protein, which is responsible for absorbing a critical for life vitamin, had to have already been in place in order for the organism to function.

The Immune System

The complement system is part of our immune defense network. It is a biochemical chain of events triggered by the human body recognizing a foreign invader and developing a multi-protein complex which will be used to poke holes into the membrane (skin/wall) of the invader. This system also informs the white blood cell, the macrophage, which invader to attack and eat (macro means big and phage means 'to eat'). Over fifteen proteins are involved in the complement cascade and this is only the beginning. Again, if one protein is missing from the cascade it fails to function. This leaves the organism vulnerable to infection after infection and eventually one of the infections will be their last.

The first part of your immune system is your skin, the largest organ in the body. This is not only a physical barrier to invaders (bacteria, fungus, parasites, viruses) but there are chemicals on your skin that help inhibit or outright kill bacteria. Many of the oils our skin produces are not only there to moisturize the skin, but trap would-be invaders, and proteins within the secretions help inhibit bacterial growth. However, one of the greatest defenders of invaders is bacteria. Yes, bacteria helping us to prevent other microbes (bacteria, fungus, parasites, viruses) from invasion. They do this by just living on our skin. Our skin is covered by billions and billions of bacteria and just by occupying space they do not allow harmful invaders to colonize our skin. The same is true for our intestinal tract (digestive system), which has pounds of bacteria in it, and even has some viruses and fungus (yeast) for good measure, but we will talk about the gastrointestinal tract later. What if the skin barrier fails or a microbe invades our nose or mouth? In the nose, our next line of defense is mucus. Microbes stick to mucus and cannot get out, they are then either sneezed, blown, or coughed out, or it drains down our throats and the stomach acid destroys them for good. In the back of the throat and mouth are the tonsils and adenoids, once thought to be vestigial organs or an organ that had a purpose millions of years ago but is not really needed anymore, play an important role in our immune system. The adenoids act like lymph nodes (discussed later) and our tonsils are somewhat similar in that they contain deep pits of which microbes fall into like a trap. While the microbes are in the tonsillar crypts (the pits) there are antibodies contained within that stick to the microbes and inhibit the microbe from invading into deeper structures. There are also white blood cells down there that kill some of the microbes and take some of the broken pieces of the microbe to different parts of the immune system (lymph nodes) in order to learn that microbe's unique chemical signature for possible future infections.

Inhaled microbes contend with mucus as well and then are carried up what we call a 'ciliary escalator.' Cilia are microscopic, hair-like parts of a cell that are designed to move things along. Think of the legs of a millipede or caterpillar but used to move things away from it while it remains stationary. In certain microorganisms cilia are used for motility. Flagella is a term for one or more exceptionally long cilia that typically move in a corkscrew fashion to propel the organism forward; examples of this are seen with sperm or the bacterium *E. coli*. Flagella are even more biochemically complex than cilia but are used for a different purpose. The cilia consist of a chain of thousands of proteins designed for movement. In the airway they help push mucus filled with inhaled foreign material, such as smoke, dust, or microbes up our wind pipes and back into our mouth where we either cough the material out or swallow it into our stomachs to be destroyed by the stomach acid.

The next line of defense is deep in the lungs themselves where the alveoli (ah-vee-oh-ly) are. Alveoli are the sacs within our lungs where the gas exchange between oxygen and carbon dioxide occur. Within the alveoli live our 'big-eaters', the macrophages. Here we call them alveolar macrophages or dust cells, in that they clear out dust but more importantly they ingest microbes and destroy them. These cells, along with basophils for allergy defense; eosinophils for allergy and parasitic infection defense; mast cells; neutrophils, and monocytes are part of our 'innate' immune system. The innate immune system is the portion of the immune system that is always on guard and ready to attack immediately, whatever may come. Allergic symptoms are simply an overreaction by basophils to what they perceive to be a threat (antigen). An antigen (ann-teh-jen) is anything the body senses as foreign material. What demonstrates their immediateness is an allergy to cat hair. When walking into a room filled with cats, how quickly does a person begin sneezing and getting watery eyes? The answer is within seconds to minutes. This is the basophils (bay-zo-fils), and to some extent the eosinophils (ee-o-sin-o-fils) reacting to the foreign protein of the cat dander. Our body encounters millions of antigens a day and yet we are not sick every day. From dust, dirt, noxious gas, viruses, bacteria, fungal spores – to other people's germs – our immune system is constantly on guard assuring these antigen invaders do us no harm.

The next obvious level involves tissue penetrance by microbes and possible blood involvement. This is accomplished by getting a cut dirty or microbes slipping past our innate immune system. Here we have natural killer cells and macrophages for indiscriminate killing of foreign invaders, but we also have a miraculous cell known as the dendritic cell, which lives within our tissue, just deep to our skin. Anything with 'dendrites' have what look like mini-tentacles and these tentacles are covered in antigen presenting proteins. Recall, an antigen is anything and everything the body does not recognize as self. So, the dendritic cell takes pieces of a destroyed bacterium, virus, parasite, or fungus up the lymphatic system and stops within a lymph node, the thymus, or the spleen. This is why your lymph nodes may be enlarged during an infection and why the doctor will attempt to feel for them; if they are enlarged, it means they are working. Oh, did I mention the process of antigen presentation is a highly preserved and coordinated activity requiring thousands of genes and hundreds of different proteins? While in the lymph node they share this antigen material with developing B or T cells. The B and T cells are part of our 'adaptive' immune system. These cells learn and remember previous infections so that the next time that specific microbe attempts to invade your body it can mount an immediate and specific defense against it. This dendritic to lymph node process or system is precisely how vaccines work. The B cells will begin making specific antibodies for that specific antigen and may eventually develop into a plasma cell, which is a cell that produces thousands and thousands of antibodies. Antibodies are small, Y-shaped proteins that are made to recognize exceedingly specific molecular signatures of invasive microbes. Four hundred gene segments cross to produce 10,000,000,000 combinations for the creation of different antibodies. This is excellent because there are millions of potential invaders. If you remove one atom, *just one atom*, from the antibody it will not function properly and even though it is in the blood stream there is technically no defense present. Thus, one can see the importance of protein synthesis. You cannot simply attach amino acid to amino acid and have a *functional* protein. There is a refined, well-tuned process to develop *functional* proteins.

Fascinatingly, while the immune system is orchestrating this robust defense, chemicals are released by immune cells that result in vasoconstriction (constricting the blood vessels) around the infection so that the infection does not spread. Simultaneously, chemicals are released to vasodilate (dilate the blood vessels) within the area of infection in order to deliver more white blood cells and nutrients for curing and healing. This typically results in an abscess that helps halt the advance of the infecting microbe. Chemicals released from white blood cells also alert our brain that we have an infection and the hypothalamus (hi-po-thal-a-mus) of the brain will reset our internal thermometer, which results in a fever. Fevers are a call to arms for the rest of the immune system and result in an unfavorable growing environment for certain microbes. These same chemicals can also make us feel tired and achy, resulting in us seeking rest, and rest is excellent for the immune system's optimal function.

The T cells are the generals of the immune system. Some are killers but the majority are immune system regulators and coordinators. They are the great logisticians of the immune system. The T cells also do self-regulatory checks of our body. For example, in response to certain infections, let us say the flu (influenza), a T cell can attach to a B cell and if there is a match, the T cell will secrete proteins called *interleukins*. The interleukins inform the brain to raise our basal temperature (produce a fever), makes us a little sleepy, and calls to arms the rest of the immune system. Sleep is excellent for the immune system and this is why rest is recommended by physicians when you are ill. When a cell is in trouble, whether by a foreign invader living inside of it or its DNA is malfunctioning, it will display an SOS code within its cell membrane (wall of the cell) and the T cell will recognize this signal. The T cell then organizes and ensures this cell is destroyed, typically by triggered apoptosis, or cell self-death. If we did not have this portion of the regulatory immune system, we would have tumors all over our body and would likely not survive past childhood without developing cancer.

I would wager the immune system is the most finicky when it comes to mutations. It does not like change. Changes in the DNA here either result in blood cancers like leukemia or lymphoma or autoimmune diseases. Auto means self, and autoimmune diseases are ailments that occur when your own immune system attacks your own cells. Some examples of this are Crohn's disease, Hashimoto's thyroiditis (hypothyroidism), lupus, and rheumatoid arthritis. If we then couple this incredibly complex system with the fact that any genetic manipulation within results in cancer or autoimmune disease, we can estimate the likelihood of this system gradually developing over millions of years to be outright improbable.

Digestion

The alimentary tract, also known as our gastrointestinal tract, involves the thirty feet of tubing from our mouth to anus; the liver, the gall bladder, the pancreas, and 100 trillion bacteria (ewwy). For one, the thirty feet of tubing is designed to absorb nutrients at certain places within the tract. Glucose (sugar) is our primary energy source and in times of hunger and low energy levels (low sugar) we need this energy as soon as possible. Well, we have a fix for this. The mouth contains enzymes that immediately process the incoming carbohydrates (fancy word for sugar) and our bodies begin absorbing them immediately. The stomach acids help break down proteins, but the pancreas is the real hero in that it releases enzymes to break down fat, proteins, and carbohydrates. Fat needs a little extra help since it is chemically unique, it must first be emulsified. Ever try putting olive oil in water or in a vinaigrette? Emulsification is a process that allows those oils (i.e. fat) to mix with the other structures so that it may be processed by the digestive system. Helping with the breakdown of fat is bile, which is made in the liver and stored in the gall bladder. Many people think the gall bladder is what is known as a vestigial organ, again, an organ that had a purpose millions of years ago but not really needed anymore. This is not only untrue, but the term has been misused for far too long. Just because one can live without an organ does not mean it is not necessary. Sure, a person can live without a spleen, but I sure wouldn't want to. It makes red blood cell recycling impossible and since it has immune functions it predisposes one to all sorts of infections. Well, the same is true for the gall bladder. Sure, we can live without it, but it is not fun. The stored bile makes it nice and easy to begin breaking down fat into fatty acids, which makes its absorption possible. Without it, fat remains in our intestines longer than it should in its normal state and this can cause malabsorption, nausea, vomiting, flatulence (passing gas), and abdominal pain.

The food or bolus marches on in our intestines, with a B vitamin being absorbed here, iron there, calcium here, and vitamin C here and so on. Interestingly we get most of our vitamin B_{12} and K via the byproducts of bacteria. Byproducts? The human byproduct of eating and metabolism is feces (poop), so the bacteria are thus taking the food we eat and 'pooping' vitamins for us to use; and in return we provide them with nutrition and a home to live in. This is called a symbiotic relationship. The prefix sym- means together or with. A symbiotic relationship is one where a species lives inside or on another species and this relationship benefits both parties. More on this in chapter six.

The food bolus travels through the longest part of the tract called the small intestines and finally meets the colon or large intestine. The intersection where the small and large intestine meet is called the ileocecal junction and once through that we are in the colon; connected to this first portion of the colon is our friend the appendix - the most picked on 'vestigial organ' of the entire human body. Again, the term vestigial infers that the structure has no more use. The appendix has at minimum two significant functions, one, is the production of several vitamins, and two, it has high concentration of lymphoid aggregations or clusters of white blood cells crucial to the immune system both for killing and learning new invaders. B cells mature here, and it is in a prime location for this. Since the appendix is at the very bottom of the colon (large intestine) gravity works to assure foreign invaders can fall into the small inner tube of the appendix with ease. This is analogous to our tonsil's crypts. The appendix is also thought to have a role in maintaining our gut flora or microbiota; names for the 100 trillion bacteria living in our intestines. Individuals without an appendix were found to be four times more likely to have a recurrence of the deadly *Clostridium difficile* colitis (inflammation of the colon) infection (*C. diff*). The reservoir of bacteria may serve a purpose in repopulating the gut bacteria after its destruction by antibiotic use or by dysentery/diarrheal infection. On top of this, the body still sees fit to supply the appendix with its own blood supply, venous drainage, and lymphatics. Ignorance of a structures function is a poor argument in any field of science.

Now that the food bolus is in the colon bacteria really go to work and begin producing all kinds of vitamins and minerals necessary for life. It is also here that water is taken out of the bolus in order to form solid stool as well as hydrate us, nothing important going to waste, pardon the pun. Our bodies are extremely efficient and leave little to be squandered. For example, the kidneys reabsorb 100 percent of the glucose (sugar) that is filtered from the blood because it is so vital to our energy production. Naturally, whatever remains ends up in our toilet bowls.

But where does all this energy, nutrients, and minerals go once they are absorbed? The digestive system has its very own venous drainage. Now this is huge, so bear with me. Most of the human body drains blood through what is called the vena caval system. This is the largest vein in the body, and it runs along our vertebral column (spinal cord) alongside the aorta, the largest artery in the human body. As stated, all blood from the entire human body (minus the heart) eventually ends up in this large vein, but the digestive organs first drain through the liver before draining into the caval system. This is called the portal system, because the vein draining all this blood into the liver is called the portal vein. The intestines from the stomach to upper portion of the rectum, spleen, pancreas, and gall bladder must all drain their blood through the portal system that then drains directly into the liver. The liver, in my humble opinion, has almost an unfair share of tasks for the human body. It seems to do everything, from making blood clotting proteins, producing blood unclotting proteins, storing glycogen (stored form of sugar), vitamins, minerals, making proteins, manufacturing the hormone thrombopoietin (throm-bo-po-ee-tin); which tells the bone marrow to make more platelets). The liver also produces bile, excretes cholesterol, recycles iron, and purifies blood. When it comes to digestion, it processes many nutrients, interacts with hormones that regulate nutrient processing, and remove toxins. Phew! The liver also begins processing most of the drugs we take orally. This is a Herculean undertaking and requires billions and billions of genetic base pairs and thousands of proteins to operate. Only when the liver has deemed these molecules fit for service in the human body are they then released out the hepatic veins (hepatic means liver) and *then* into the vena caval system. This means that special and unique transcription factors had to be made in order to assure the blood of the digestive system does not drain into the vena caval system but rather head to the liver. The portal system deals with an astonishing 2,000 liters (528 gallons) of blood per day. Without a liver we die. From an evolutionary standpoint a gradual evolution of a liver makes absolutely no sense. Our liverless ancestors would die within a day or two, and no, not from cowardice. Of course, they would have never made it to birth because whereas the red blood cells are made in the bone marrow of the adult, in the fetus they are made by the liver.

The Sun and Sapiens

The sun is the originating source of energy for every living thing on the planet. Every living organism from the oak tree to the giraffe can trace its energy source back to the sun. The sun grows the plants, the giraffe eats the plant, and a lion eats the giraffe. However, the sun also plays a pivotal role in our own health, especially our bone health. I am sorry, did he just say bone health and the sun? I sure did. Vitamin D is thought to be involved in dozens of biological functions but its most well-known function is as a crucial biomolecule for the absorption of calcium from the intestines, which is crucial for thousands of cellular processes; most famously for bone health. By the way, vitamins do nothing on their own, they are helpers for cellular processes and functions. Still critical, and we can have disease or die without them, but they do nothing on their own. Back to bones. Bone gives our body structure, support, and supply a structure onto which our muscles attach to so we can be mobile. Bone is also the massive storage source of calcium for our body. Calcium is crucial for muscle contraction, heart contractions, and neurological signaling. If the body thinks it is a bit low on calcium it will release a hormone (parathyroid hormone) that tells the bone to release more calcium into the bloodstream. Vitamin D production is dependent on the sun. There are very few food sources that supply vitamin D. Even most milk products with vitamin D in it are a result of us adding vitamin D to the milk. Ironically, mushrooms are a good, natural source of vitamin D and they are grown in caves where sunlight is absent. One cup of vitamin D milk contains 115 – 130 international units (IU) of vitamin D and our bodies daily need is 400 IU, so the sun is important in meeting this goal. In shorts and a t-shirt, you only need ten to fifteen minutes of sunlight to achieve your daily requirement of vitamin D. The sun achieves this for us by its ultraviolet radiation penetrating our skin, then through the blood vessel wall, to hit the biomolecule 7-dehydrocholesterol (dee-hi-dro-kul-es-ter-ol) which turns it into the molecule cholecalciferol (kol-kal-sif-er-ol). The liver then converts cholecalciferol into 25-hydroxycholecalciferol (hi-drox-ee-kol-kal-sif-er-ol). The liver also regulates the feedback of this pre-vitamin to assure we do not get excessive levels of vitamin D. The liver can also store 25-hydroxycholecalciferol for later use when levels seem a bit low. The 25-hydroxycholecalciferol is then finally converted into 1,25-dihydrocholecalciferol (die-hi-dro-kol-kal-sif-er-ol), also known as vitamin D_3 which is the official, active form of vitamin D! Phew, we made it. Oh, and this final form is converted within the kidneys and is under the influence of parathyroid (pair-a-thy-roid) hormone. Sun, skin, blood, liver, and kidneys make vitamin D synthesis possible. No vitamin D and our bones soften, which is eventually followed by symptoms of low calcium including confusion, muscle spasms, numbness, tingling, depression, hallucinations, abnormal heart rhythms, seizures, and eventually death. Can someone please explain to me how this evolved slowly over time? What did we do before this evolved? What if we had the kidneys but no liver? Did our ancestors walk around with low calcium levels and die in infanthood? My point being that this complex system had to have been established for our life to exist and thus, either had to be created from the start or not. Incredible to ponder, something 93,000,000 miles away is important for our bone health, the deepest structure of our limbs.

Energy

Eating and subsequent absorption have occurred in the previous section, now we must take these organic products and turn them into energy because cellular processes require energy. You cannot conduct the turnover of over a trillion atoms every one billionth of a second without using energy. For humans, and obviously many other creatures, we take in food, water, and oxygen, and as a result of metabolism, give off the breakdown products carbon dioxide and heat. Plants take in radiative energy from the sun, carbon dioxide, and water. Photons (light particles) split the carbon dioxide, the carbon portion goes to build the plant and the oxygen is expelled. Plants metabolic byproduct is oxygen. Eventually they die, and their remains rot away, turning mostly back into carbon dioxide, nitrogen, and water, which conveniently is used as fertilizer for future generations of plants and a food source for nature's recyclers, the saprophages (i.e. mushrooms, worms, bacteria). Picture saprophages (sa-pro-fajes) as the vultures of the plant world, however they achieve immeasurably more benefit to the planet Earth.

Plants use an energy cycle called the Calvin cycle and in humans (animals) it is called the Kreb's cycle also known as the citric acid cycle. The citric acid cycle is a complex cycle utilizing eight key enzymes, and ten steps to turn acetyl-CoA (a-see-tul-ko-ā) molecules into a source of electrons for the mitochondria (powerhouse of the cell) organelle. While there, they are used to produce adenosine (a-den-o-sin) triphosphate (ATP), our primary energy molecule that makes our muscles contract and carries out trillions of proteinaceous processes every second. The human body turns over its weight in ATP daily. The acetyl-CoA molecule came from the breakdown of a glucose (sugar) molecule in a process known as glycolysis (gly-kol-eh-sis). As previously stated, the goal is to get molecules rich in electrons that can be used in the electron transport chain within the mitochondria. Recall, the electrons are the rapidly moving 'cloud' around the nucleus of an atom. It is the smallest subparticle of the atom. Imagine that phenomenon, humans with their trillions of cells and extraordinarily complex organ systems, use the smallest subatomic particle for energy production.

The eight enzymes involved in the citric acid cycle (Kreb's cycle) are all irreducibly complex and thus crucially necessary. If just one enzyme is not there then every step thereafter does not occur, no energy production and you have rigor mortis and death. Remember our friend the odds one to 10^{164th} power to denote the chance of a 150 amino acid sized protein randomly evolving? What if we were then to take this number and apply the odds of just the eight of these enzymes randomly evolving? And recall that a 150 amino acid protein is a small protein. One of the eight enzymes is *isocitrate dehydrogenase*, which is over 400 amino acids in size. We have not even discussed the mitochondrial membrane proteins that allow the electron transport chain to accomplish its goals. To picture a more accurate number we would have to more than double the 10^{164} odds for just one of the eight enzymes! Let us see a number with 164 zeros in it just so we have a good picture … 100,000,000,000,000,000,0 00,000,000,000,000,000,000,000,000,000,000,000,000,000,000 ,000,000,000,000,000,000,000,000,000,000,000,000,000,000,0 00,000,000,000,000,000,000,000,000,000,000,000,000,000,000 ,000,000,000,000,000.

One could argue that perhaps early animals may have just used lactate as an energy source? Incorrect. Lactate or lactic acid is produced as a result of anaerobic metabolism, anaerobic meaning no oxygen is present. This lactic acid is the soreness in the muscle you feel after an intense work out. The problem with this is not only is it inefficient, but it still must be converted into a molecule called pyruvate that via an enzymatic reaction becomes acetyl-CoA and thus enters the citric acid cycle. This energy production is yet another irreducibly complex system in which had to exist in its current and perfect form in order to sustain the energy necessary for human life.

Six

SMALL OLD LIFE

Entire volumes containing thousands of pages have been written on microorganisms. The field of study being microbiology. Here, I will mainly be discussing the microbe's role as it pertains to our existence. If you took all the bacteria in existence it would weigh more than every single animal on Earth combined, including insects. As a matter of fact, they would outweigh us by a factor of 35. Their cumulative weight is 1,116 times more massive than all the humans combined. As stated earlier, you have four pounds of bacteria in your large intestines alone.

Recall, bacteria helps us to prevent other microbes (bacteria, fungus, parasites, viruses) from invading us just by merely existing on us and within us. Our gut bacteria also help regulate many of our hormones. Many scientists and physicians are even beginning to argue for treating the gut microbiota as its own organ system. Our overuse of antibiotics is one of the many explanations given for our increase in the number of autoimmune and hyperimmune related disorders, including our surge in asthma cases. We consume many invasive microbes daily. Yes, many are inhaled, but more are consumed. Well, our system leaves nothing to waste. From the tonsils all the way through the intestines, white blood cells and lymphatics are busily working to learn the microbes that were ingested so that if they ever invade our bodies, we will be ready to destroy them. Interestingly, our body learns the good bacteria in our intestines but ensures they are not destroyed. Due to the incredible number of antigens (foreign material) we consume one could argue the intestinal immune system is one of the largest portions of the entire immune system. Thus, it makes sense that when we disrupt this microbiota with antibiotics or 'bubble theory,' disease may arise. Bubble theory is a colloquial term to describe the phenomenon of children growing up never playing outside, excessively using hand sanitizer, and eating unpasteurized food. These things decrease the exposure to antigens and microbes resulting in weakened or at minimum, immature immune systems. This leads to more allergies, asthma, and autoimmune disease. The gut microbiota is a crucial symbiotic partner for our immune system.

The bacteria on and within us play a crucial role in our life cycle and health. Bacteria within our gut produce, as their byproducts, vitamins, and not just any vitamins, but ones crucial to our existence. Recall, vitamins like vitamin B_{12} for our blood cell and brain health, as well as vitamin K, which is crucial in making the proteins that regulate our blood clotting system. Now before our cells and their cells (bacteria) got together, talked to one another, and decided they should work together, how did we survive?

Microorganisms in the ocean produce more than double the Earth's atmospheric oxygen. As a matter of fact, phytoplankton, and aquatic plants (e.g. kelp, algae, seaweed) produce seventy percent of the Earth's oxygen. Take that, Brazilian rain forest. Even bacteria get in on the action. *Cyanobacteria* is a water bacterium that produces oxygen from photosynthesis. Wait, even bacteria are getting in on the carbon dioxide and oxygen regulation of Earth's climate? They sure are!

Bacteria, from an evolutionary standpoint, were the first organisms. They were around for 2 billion years before any of us roamed the Earth, yet it is us who ponder the soul and not *E. coli*. Why are we not bowing to our bacterial masters? Why is it us sending women and men to space but not *Staphylococcus aureus*?

Old Life

We discussed the Cambrian explosion earlier and how the atmosphere changed drastically almost overnight, which was subsequently followed by the fossil record revealing dozens of different body types. If gradual evolution were a good working theory, there would be very similar body types emerging through each period within the strata (layers) of the Earth's crust. The Precambrian era contains microfossils of single celled organisms. Bacteria had a 2,000,000,000-year head start on us, according to the theory of evolution, yet there are no intermediates from microbe to insect like creatures.

There are an estimated 8.7 million species that exist right now, but ninety-nine percent of all species that have *ever* existed are extinct ($\approx 10^9$). But to say a caveman was simply a separate species of primate as opposed to a precursor to *homo sapiens* is completely verboten in the scientific community. Especially when we live in a time where there are roughly 300 primate species. Why do bones in a cave have to be a precursor and not just another species? The models you see in a museum typically have less hair than a chimp but more than us. There is no fossil evidence of this. They may very well have been completely covered in hair. Just for far stretches of funny hypotheses; what if the only 300 skeletons of the Neanderthals (cavemen) we have discovered were simply humans who were outcast from society for their abnormal look? Perhaps they had acromegaly (think Andre the Giant)? (Insert laugh here). Maybe not say that about Andre?

The two types of cavemen that are discussed the most are Cro-Magnon and Neanderthal. The Cro-Magnon skeleton is the one who has a skeleton most similar to us *homo sapiens*. However, Cro-Magnon is not thought to have evolved from Neanderthal. Oh, and did I mention, the fossil record is absent of a relative for pre-Cro-Magnon. The supposed evolutionary split from us and chimpanzees took place only 7 million years ago. Remember all of those calculations of how nearly impossible it is to form random proteins or sustain genetic changes? Well now we have only 7 million years to make a modern human. Genetic information is packaged in chromosomes and collectively known as the genome. In genetic movements from cell to cell, and from generation to generation, three percent of the genome is 'active.' This is approximately 90 million base pairs of DNA. Let us suppose there is only a one percent difference between us (*homo sapiens*) and the Cro-Magnon ancestor. One percent of 90 million is 900,000. So, we have only 7 million years to make 900,000 changes to the genome. Again, please refer to the calculations in chapters three and four to realize how incredibly impossible this is. Only 300 Neanderthal remains have been found and none are 100 percent intact. Neanderthals also apparently walked side by side with us for 70,000 years yet there is no mention of them nor very many preserved skeletons. They have also only been found in Europe and some parts of the Middle East, and these skeletons are only 40,000 to 130,000 years old. Meanwhile, we have approximately 2,100 dinosaur skeletons and have a working knowledge of 300 to 500 different species of dinosaur, yet they all died 65 million years ago. Most peculiar. Any honest comparative anatomist or forensic pathologist will tell you there are skeletal differences between different ethnic groups. Why, then, are we so quick to label a fossil skeleton found in the ground to be a human precursor and why could it not just be another species of primate?

Fun fact, the human foot is the most unique anatomical structure of the human body. The primates have many similarities with us anatomically, but the human foot is completely unique. It is what makes us bipedal (walks on two limbs). And as much as Darwinists love to jump up and down when they see a gorilla walk on two legs it is still a quadruped (walks on four limbs) at the end of the day. Interestingly, we have no completely intact Neanderthal foot. There is an estimated 230 to 270 species of primates and none of them have the human foot.

When you realize genes primarily code for proteins it does

become slightly less amazing that we share similar DNA with other species. If it is not broke, do not fix it. I would add this to the discussion, "natural selection lacks intention." How do cells that have no cellular thinking dictate the DNA to change? For example, let us imagine the climate is getting colder. Having more hair or more fat may help the species out. Who makes this decision? A liver cell? Skin cell? Brain cell? Who or what makes this decision? Recall the vast majority of genetic changes are bad for the organism. It is the equivalent of 'Nature' reaching into a bag of 10^{390} protein possibilities, chose one that worked, and repeated it a trillion times! The esteemed scientist Dr. Gerald Schroeder, summarized the Neo-Darwinists reasoning for random mutations as "nature's challenges then selected for or against the change expressed." And he is correct, how did nature do the selecting? What is the biochemical signal for that choice? The cell has no conscience to make decisions, especially complex biomolecule decisions. Even if this "decision" is made, then is the genetic trait recessive or dominant? For example, brown eyes or black hair is more likely to be expressed in offspring because the gene for those colors is more dominant. And the change then must be expressed in the sex cells (gametes), known as sperm and ova (eggs). Mutations occur in one in ten cell divisions (again, most are bad and subsequently corrected), but gamete cell mutations occur one in every 100,000. Gametes are determined to maintain the status quo. They dislike change for they must propagate the species. Let us go to another level down and remind one that you now must pass that one change, in one individual's gametes and distribute them among the entire species. If not lost, the change may take 5,000 generations to finally affect the entire species. Even with all perfect scenarios being met with consistent and dependable changes in the DNA it would take hundreds of millions of generations to occur. When the first fish left the ocean with its new limbs, some thought it better to become a salamander and yet some went forth to become an elephant. Was there a source of disagreement with the cells and their DNA about which species was better to become? At the end of the day the fossil record is the only "evidence" and with its lack of indispensable transitional intermediates, even it fails to confirm their theory.

This text is merely a pebble drop of what is the complexity of our existence. We have discussed how the solar system, sun, and moon all play a crucial role in our existence. We have discussed the intricacies of molecules and the cells. So, what are the complete statistical odds of life randomly forming and functioning? Well, it is one in 100000000000000000000000000000000000000000000 0000000000000000000000000000000000000000000000

0000000000000000000000000000000000000000000000000
0000000000000000000000000000000000000000000000000
0000000000000000000000000000000000000000000000000
0000000000000000000000000000000000000000000000000
0000000000000000000000000000000000000000000000000
0000000000000000000000000000000000000000000000000
0000000000000000000000000000000000000000000000000
0000000000000000000000000000000000000000000000000
0000000000000000000000000000000000000000000000000
0000000000000000000000000000000000000000000000000
0000000000000000000000000000000000000000000000000
0000000000000000000000000000000000000000000000000
0000000000000000000000000000000000000000000000000
0000000000000000000000000000000000000000000000000
0000000000000000000000000000000000000000000000000
0000000000000000000000000000000000000000000000000
0000000000000000000000000000000000000000000000000
0000000000000000000000000000000000000000000000000
0000000000000000000000000000000000000000000000000
0000000000000000000000000000000000000000000000000
0000000000000000000000000000000000000000000000000
0000000000000000000000000000000000000000000000000
0000000000000000000000000000000000000000000000000
0000000000000000000000000000000000000000000000000
0000000000000000000000000000000000000000000000000
0000000000000000000000000000000000000000000000000
0000000000000000000000000000000000000000000000000
0000000000000000000000000000000000000000000000000
0000000000000000000000000000000000000000000000000
0000000000000000000000000000000000000000000000000
0000000000000000000000000000000000000000000000000
0000000000000000000000000000000000000000000000000
0000000000000000000000000000000000000000000000000
0000000000000000000000000000000000000000000000000
0000000000000000000000000000000000000000000000000
0000000000000000000000000000000000000000000000000
0000000000000000000000000000000000000000000000000

000000000000000000000000000000000000000000000000000000
000000000000000000000000000000000000000000000000000000
000000000000000000000000000000000000000000000000000000
000000000000000000000000000000000000000000000000000000
000000000000000000000000000000000000000000000000000000
000000000000000000000000000000000000000000000000000000
000000000000000000000000000000000000000000000000000000
000000000000000000000000000000000000000000000000000000
000000000000000000000000000000000000000000000000000000
000000000000000000000000000000000000000000000000000000
000000000000000000000000000000000000000000000000000000
000000000000000000000000000000000000000000000000000000
000000000000000000000000000000000000000000000000000000
000000000000000000000000000000000000000000000000000000
000000000000000000000000000000000000000000000000000000
000000000000000000000000000000000000000000000000000000
000000000000000000000000000000000000000000000000000000
000000000000000000000000000000000000000000000000000000
000000000000000000000000000000000000000000000000000000
000000000000000000000000000000000000000000000000000000
000000000000000000000000000000000000000000000000000000
000000000000000000000000000000000000000000000000000000
000000000000000000000000000000000000000000000000000000
000000000000000000000000000000000000000000000000000000
000000000000000000000000000000000000000000000000000000
000000000000000000000000000000000000000000000000000000
000000000000000000000000000000000000000000000000000000
000000000000000000000000000000000000000000000000000000
000000000000000000000000000000000000000000000000000000
000000000000000000000000000000000000000000000000000000
000000000000000000000000000000000000000000000000000000
000000000000000000000000000000000000000000000000000000
000000000000000000000000000000000000000000000000000000
000000000000000000000000000000000000000000000000000000
000000000000000000000000000000000000000000000000000000
000000000000000000000000000000000000000000000000000000
000000000000000000000000000000000000000000000000000000
000000000000000000000000000000000000000000000000000000

0000000000000000000000000000000000000000000000000
0000000000000000000000000000000000000000000000000
0000000000000000000000000000000000000000000000000
0000000000000000000000000000000000000000000000000
0000000000000000000000000000000000000000000000000
0000000000000000000000000000000000000000000000000
0000000000000000000000000000000000000000000000000
0000000000000000000000000000000000000000000000000
0000000000000000000000000000000000000000000000000
0000000000000000000000000000000000000000000000000
0000000000000000000000000000000000000000000000000
0000000000000000000000000000000000000000000000000
0000000000000000000000000000000000000000000000000
0000000000000000000000000000000000000000000000000
0000000000000000000000000000000000000000000000000
0000000000000000000000000000000000000000000000000
0000000000000000000000000000000000000000000000000
0000000000000000000000000000000000000000000000000
0000000000000000000000000000000000000000000000000
0000000000000000000000000000000000000000000000000
0000000000000000000000000000000000000000000000000
0000000000000000000000000000000000000000000000000
0000000000000000000000000000000000000000000000000
0000000000000000000000000000000000000000000000000
0000000000000000000000000000000000000000000000000
0000000000000000000000000000000000000000000000000
0000000000000000000000000000000000000000000000000
0000000000000000000000000000000000000000000000000
0000000000000000000000000000000000000000000000000
0000000000000000000000000000000000000000000000000
0000000000000000000000000000000000000000000000000
0000000000000000000000000000000000000000000000000
0000000000000000000000000000000000000000000000000
0000000000000000000000000000000000000000000000000
0000000000000000000000000000000000000000000000000

00000000000000000000000000000000000000000000000000000
00000000000000000000000000000000000000000000000000000
00000000000000000000000000000000000000000000000000000
00000000000000000000000000000000000000000000000000000
00000000000000000000000000000000000000000000000000000
00000000000000000000000000000000000000000000000000000
00000000000000000000000000000000000000000000000000000
00000000000000000000000000000000000000000000000000000
00000000000000000000000000000000000000000000000000000
00000000000000000000000000000000000000000000000000000
00000000000000000000000000000000000000000000000000000
00000000000000000000000000000000000000000000000000000
00000000000000000000000000000000000000000000000000000
00000000000000000000000000000000000000000000000000000
00000000000000000000000000000000000000000000000000000
00000000000000000000000000000000000000000000000000000
00000000000000000000000000000000000000000000000000000
00000000000000000000000000000000000000000000000000000
00000000000000000000000000000000000000000000000000000
00000000000000000000000000000000000000000000000000000
00000000000000000000000000000000000000000000000000000
00000000000000000000000000000000000000000000000000000
00000000000000000000000000000000000000000000000000000
00000000000000000000000000000000000000000000000000000
00000000000000000000000000000000000000000000000000000
00000000000000000000000000000000000000000000000000000
00000000000000000000000000000000000000000000000000000
00000000000000000000000000000000000000000000000000000
00000000000000000000000000000000000000000000000000000
00000000000000000000000000000000000000000000000000000
00000000000000000000000000000000000000000000000000000
00000000000000000000000000000000000000000000000000000
00000000000000000000000000000000000000000000000000000
00000000000000000000000000000000000000000000000000000
00000000000000000000000000000000000000000000000000000
00000000000000000000000000000000000000000000000000000
00000000000000000000000000000000000000000000000000000

0000000000000000000000000000000000000000000000000000
0000000000000000000000000000000000000000000000000000
0000000000000000000000000000000000000000000000000000
0000000000000000000000000000000000000000000000000000
0000000000000000000000000000000000000000000000000000
0000000000000000000000000000000000000000000000000000
0000000000000000000000000000000000000000000000000000
0000000000000000000000000000000000000000000000000000
0000000000000000000000000000000000000000000000000000
0000000000000000000000000000000000000000000000000000
0000000000000000000000000000000000000000000000000000
0000000000000000000000000000000000000000000000000000
0000000000000000000000000000000000000000000000000000
0000000000000000000000000000000000000000000000000000
0000000000000000000000000000000000000000000000000000
0000000000000000000000000000000000000000000000000000
0000000000000000000000000000000000000000000000000000
0000000000000000000000000000000000000000000000000000
0000000000000000000000000000000000000000000000000000
0000000000000000000000000000000000000000000000000000
0000000000000000000000000000000000000000000000000000
0000000000000000000000000000000000000000000000000000
0000000000000000000000000000000000000000000000000000
0000000000000000000000000000000000000000000000000000
0000000000000000000000000000000000000000000000000000
0000000000000000000000000000000000000000000000000000
0000000000000000000000000000000000000000000000000000
0000000000000000000000000000000000000000000000000000
0000000000000000000000000000000000000000000000000000
0000000000000000000000000000000000000000000000000000
0000000000000000000000000000000000000000000000000000
0000000000000000000000000000000000000000000000000000
0000000000000000000000000000000000000000000000000000
0000000000000000000000000000000000000000000000000000
0000000000000000000000000000000000000000000000000000
0000000000000000000000000000000000000000000000000000
0000000000000000000000000000000000000000000000000000

DR. JAMES KINDLUND

000000000000000000000000000000000000000000000000000000
000000000000000000000000000000000000000000000000000000
000000000000000000000000000000000000000000000000000000
000000000000000000000000000000000000000000000000000000
000000000000000000000000000000000000000000000000000000
000000000000000000000000000000000000000000000000000000
000000000000000000000000000000000000000000000000000000
000000000000000000000000000000000000000000000000000000
000000000000000000000000000000000000000000000000000000
000000000000000000000000000000000000000000000000000000
000000000000000000000000000000000000000000000000000000
000000000000000000000000000000000000000000000000000000
000000000000000000000000000000000000000000000000000000
000000000000000000000000000000000000000000000000000000
000000000000000000000000000000000000000000000000000000
000000000000000000000000000000000000000000000000000000
000000000000000000000000000000000000000000000000000000
000000000000000000000000000000000000000000000000000000
000000000000000000000000000000000000000000000000000000
000000000000000000000000000000000000000000000000000000
000000000000000000000000000000000000000000000000000000
000000000000000000000000000000000000000000000000000000
000000000000000000000000000000000000000000000000000000
000000000000000000000000000000000000000000000000000000
000000000000000000000000000000000000000000000000000000
000000000000000000000000000000000000000000000000000000
000000000000000000000000000000000000000000000000000000
000000000000000000000000000000000000000000000000000000
000000000000000000000000000000000000000000000000000000
000000000000000000000000000000000000000000000000000000
000000000000000000000000000000000000000000000000000000
000000000000000000000000000000000000000000000000000000
000000000000000000000000000000000000000000000000000000
000000000000000000000000000000000000000000000000000000
000000000000000000000000000000000000000000000000000000
000000000000000000000000000000000000000000000000000000
000000000000000000000000000000000000000000000000000000

0000000000000000000000000000000000000000000000000000
0000000000000000000000000000000000000000000000000000
0000000000000000000000000000000000000000000000000000
0000000000000000000000000000000000000000000000000000
0000000000000000000000000000000000000000000000000000
0000000000000000000000000000000000000000000000000000
0000000000000000000000000000000000000000000000000000
0000000000000000000000000000000000000000000000000000
0000000000000000000000000000000000000000000000000000
0000000000000000000000000000000000000000000000000000
0000000000000000000000000000000000000000000000000000
0000000000000000000000000000000000000000000000000000
0000000000000000000000000000000000000000000000000000
0000000000000000000000000000000000000000000000000000
0000000000000000000000000000000000000000000000000000
0000000000000000000000000000000000000000000000000000
0000000000000000000000000000000000000000000000000000
0000000000000000000000000000000000000000000000000000
0000000000000000000000000000000000000000000000000000
0000000000000000000000000000000000000000000000000000
0000000000000000000000000000000000000000000000000000
0000000000000000000000000000000000000000000000000000
0000000000000000000000000000000000000000000000000000
0000000000000000000000000000000000000000000000000000
0000000000000000000000000000000000000000000000000000
0000000000000000000000000000000000000000000000000000
0000000000000000000000000000000000000000000000000000
0000000000000000000000000000000000000000000000000000
0000000000000000000000000000000000000000000000000000
0000000000000000000000000000000000000000000000000000
0000000000000000000000000000000000000000000000000000
0000000000000000000000000000000000000000000000000000
0000000000000000000000000000000000000000000000000000
0000000000000000000000000000000000000000000000000000
0000000000000000000000000000000000000000000000000000
0000000000000000000000000000000000000000000000000000
0000000000000000000000000000000000000000000000000000

0000000000000000000000000000000000000000000000000000
0000000000000000000000000000000000000000000000000000
0000000000000000000000000000000000000000000000000000
0000000000000000000000000000000000000000000000000000
0000000000000000000000000000000000000000000000000000
0000000000000000000000000000000000000000000000000000
0000000000000000000000000000000000000000000000000000
0000000000000000000000000000000000000000000000000000
0000000000000000000000000000000000000000000000000000
0000000000000000000000000000000000000000000000000000
0000000000000000000000000000000000000000000000000000
0000000000000000000000000000000000000000000000000000
0000000000000000000000000000000000000000000000000000
0000000000000000000000000000000000000000000000000000
0000000000000000000000000000000000000000000000000000
0000000000000000000000000000000000000000000000000000
0000000000000000000000000000000000000000000000000000
0000000000000000000000000000000000000000000000000000
0000000000000000000000000000000000000000000000000000
0000000000000000000000000000000000000000000000000000
0000000000000000000000000000000000000000000000000000
0000000000000000000000000000000000000000000000000000
0000000000000000000000000000000000000000000000000000
0000000000000000000000000000000000000000000000000000
0000000000000000000000000000000000000000000000000000
0000000000000000000000000000000000000000000000000000
0000000000000000000000000000000000000000000000000000
0000000000000000000000000000000000000000000000000000
0000000000000000000000000000000000000000000000000000
0000000000000000000000000000000000000000000000000000
0000000000000000000000000000000000000000000000000000
0000000000000000000000000000000000000000000000000000
0000000000000000000000000000000000000000000000000000
0000000000000000000000000000000000000000000000000000
0000000000000000000000000000000000000000000000000000
0000000000000000000000000000000000000000000000000000

0000000000000000000000000000000000000000000000000000
0000000000000000000000000000000000000000000000000000
0000000000000000000000000000000000000000000000000000
0000000000000000000000000000000000000000000000000000
0000000000000000000000000000000000000000000000000000
0000000000000000000000000000000000000000000000000000
0000000000000000000000000000000000000000000000000000
0000000000000000000000000000000000000000000000000000
0000000000000000000000000000000000000000000000000000
0000000000000000000000000000000000000000000000000000
0000000000000000000000000000000000000000000000000000
0000000000000000000000000000000000000000000000000000
0000000000000000000000000000000000000000000000000000
0000000000000000000000000000000000000000000000000000
0000000000000000000000000000000000000000000000000000
0000000000000000000000000000000000000000000000000000
0000000000000000000000000000000000000000000000000000
0000000000000000000000000000000000000000000000000000
0000000000000000000000000000000000000000000000000000
0000000000000000000000000000000000000000000000000000
0000000000000000000000000000000000000000000000000000
0000000000000000000000000000000000000000000000000000
0000000000000000000000000000000000000000000000000000
0000000000000000000000000000000000000000000000000000
0000000000000000000000000000000000000000000000000000
0000000000000000000000000000000000000000000000000000
0000000000000000000000000000000000000000000000000000
0000000000000000000000000000000000000000000000000000
0000000000000000000000000000000000000000000000000000
0000000000000000000000000000000000000000000000000000
0000000000000000000000000000000000000000000000000000
0000000000000000000000000000000000000000000000000000
0000000000000000000000000000000000000000000000000000
0000000000000000000000000000000000000000000000000000
0000000000000000000000000000000000000000000000000000
0000000000000000000000000000000000000000000000000000
0000000000000000000000000000000000000000000000000000
0000000000000000000000000000000000000000000000000000

0000000000000000000000000000000000000000000000000000
0000000000000000000000000000000000000000000000000000
0000000000000000000000000000000000000000000000000000
0000000000000000000000000000000000000000000000000000
0000000000000000000000000000000000000000000000000000
0000000000000000000000000000000000000000000000000000
0000000000000000000000000000000000000000000000000000
0000000000000000000000000000000000000000000000000000
0000000000000000000000000000000000000000000000000000
0000000000000000000000000000000000000000000000000000
0000000000000000000000000000000000000000000000000000
0000000000000000000000000000000000000000000000000000
0000000000000000000000000000000000000000000000000000
0000000000000000000000000000000000000000000000000000
0000000000000000000000000000000000000000000000000000
0000000000000000000000000000000000000000000000000000
0000000000000000000000000000000000000000000000000000
0000000000000000000000000000000000000000000000000000
0000000000000000000000000000000000000000000000000000
0000000000000000000000000000000000000000000000000000
0000000000000000000000000000000000000000000000000000
0000000000000000000000000000000000000000000000000000
0000000000000000000000000000000000000000000000000000
0000000000000000000000000000000000000000000000000000
0000000000000000000000000000000000000000000000000000
0000000000000000000000000000000000000000000000000000
0000000000000000000000000000000000000000000000000000
0000000000000000000000000000000000000000000000000000
0000000000000000000000000000000000000000000000000000
0000000000000000000000000000000000000000000000000000
0000000000000000000000000000000000000000000000000000
0000000000000000000000000000000000000000000000000000
0000000000000000000000000000000000000000000000000000
0000000000000000000000000000000000000000000000000000

0000000000000000000000000000000000000000000000000
0000000000000000000000000000000000000000000000000
0000000000000000000000000000000000000000000000000
0000000000000000000000000000000000000000000000000
0000000000000000000000000000000000000000000000000
0000000000000000000000000000000000000000000000000
0000000000000000000000000000000000000000000000000
0000000000000000000000000000000000000000000000000
0000000000000000000000000000000000000000000000000
0000000000000000000000000000000000000000000000000
0000000000000000000000000000000000000000000000000
0000000000000000000000000000000000000000000000000
0000000000000000000000000000000000000000000000000
0000000000000000000000000000000000000000000000000
0000000000000000000000000000000000000000000000000
0000000000000000000000000000000000000000000000000
0000000000000000000000000000000000000000000000000
0000000000000000000000000000000000000000000000000
0000000000000000000000000000000000000000000000000
0000000000000000000000000000000000000000000000000
0000000000000000000000000000000000000000000000000
0000000000000000000000000000000000000000000000000
0000000000000000000000000000000000000000000000000
0000000000000000000000000000000000000000000000000
0000000000000000000000000000000000000000000000000
0000000000000000000000000000000000000000000000000
0000000000000000000000000000000000000000000000000
0000000000000000000000000000000000000000000000000
0000000000000000000000000000000000000000000000000
0000000000000000000000000000000000000000000000000
0000000000000000000000000000000000000000000000000
0000000000000000000000000000000000000000000000000
0000000000000000000000000000000000000000000000000
0000000000000000000000000000000000000000000000000
0000000000000000000000000000000000000000000000000
0000000000000000000000000000000000000000000000000

```
000000000000000000000000000000000000000000000000000
000000000000000000000000000000000000000000000000000
000000000000000000000000000000000000000000000000000
000000000000000000000000000000000000000000000000000
000000000000000000000000000000000000000000000000000
000000000000000000000000000000000000000000000000000
000000000000000000000000000000000000000000000000000
000000000000000000000000000000000000000000000000000
000000000000000000000000000000000000000000000000000
000000000000000000000000000000000000000000000000000
000000000000000000000000000000000000000000000000000
000000000000000000000000000000000000000000000000000
000000000000000000000000000000000000000000000000000
000000000000000000000000000000000000000000000000000
000000000000000000000000000000000000000000000000000
000000000000000000000000000000000000000000000000000
000000000000000000000000000000000000000000000000000
000000000000000000000000000000000000000000000000000
000000000000000000000000000000000000000000000000000
000000000000000000000000000000000000000000000000000
000000000000000000000000000000000000000000000000000
000000000000000000000000000000000000000000000000000
000000000000000000000000000000000000000000000000000
000000000000000000000000000000000000000000000000000
000000000000000000000000000000000000000000000000000
000000000000000000000000000000000000000000000000000
000000000000000000000000000000000000000000000000000
000000000000000000000000000000000000000000000000000
000000000000000000000000000000000000000000000000000
000000000000000000000000000000000000000000000000000
000000000000000000000000000000000000000000000000000
000000000000000000000000000000000000000000000000000
000000000000000000000000000000000000000000000000000
000000000000000000000000000000000000000000000000000
000000000000000000000000000000000000000000000000000
```

0000000000000000000000000000000000000000000000000000
0000000000000000000000000000000000000000000000000000
0000000000000000000000000000000000000000000000000000
0000000000000000000000000000000000000000000000000000
0000000000000000000000000000000000000000000000000000
0000000000000000000000000000000000000000000000000000
0000000000000000000000000000000000000000000000000000
0000000000000000000000000000000000000000000000000000
0000000000000000000000000000000000000000000000000000
0000000000000000000000000000000000000000000000000000
0000000000000000000000000000000000000000000000000000
0000000000000000000000000000000000000000000000000000
0000000000000000000000000000000000000000000000000000
0000000000000000000000000000000000000000000000000000
0000000000000000000000000000000000000000000000000000
0000000000000000000000000000000000000000000000000000
0000000000000000000000000000000000000000000000000000
0000000000000000000000000000000000000000000000000000
0000000000000000000000000000000000000000000000000000
0000000000000000000000000000000000000000000000000000
0000000000000000000000000000000000000000000000000000
0000000000000000000000000000000000000000000000000000
0000000000000000000000000000000000000000000000000000
0000000000000000000000000000000000000000000000000000
0000000000000000000000000000000000000000000000000000
0000000000000000000000000000000000000000000000000000
0000000000000000000000000000000000000000000000000000
0000000000000000000000000000000000000000000000000000
0000000000000000000000000000000000000000000000000000
0000000000000000000000000000000000000000000000000000
0000000000000000000000000000000000000000000000000000
0000000000000000000000000000000000000000000000000000
0000000000000000000000000000000000000000000000000000
0000000000000000000000000000000000000000000000000000
0000000000000000000000000000000000000000000000000000
0000000000000000000000000000000000000000000000000000
0000000000000000000000000000000000000000000000000000

DR. JAMES KINDLUND

000000000000000000000000000000000000000000000000000000
000000000000000000000000000000000000000000000000000000
000000000000000000000000000000000000000000000000000000
000000000000000000000000000000000000000000000000000000
000000000000000000000000000000000000000000000000000000
000000000000000000000000000000000000000000000000000000
000000000000000000000000000000000000000000000000000000
000000000000000000000000000000000000000000000000000000
000000000000000000000000000000000000000000000000000000
000000000000000000000000000000000000000000000000000000
000000000000000000000000000000000000000000000000000000
000000000000000000000000000000000000000000000000000000
000000000000000000000000000000000000000000000000000000
000000000000000000000000000000000000000000000000000000
000000000000000000000000000000000000000000000000000000
000000000000000000000000000000000000000000000000000000
000000000000000000000000000000000000000000000000000000
000000000000000000000000000000000000000000000000000000
000000000000000000000000000000000000000000000000000000
000000000000000000000000000000000000000000000000000000
000000000000000000000000000000000000000000000000000000
000000000000000000000000000000000000000000000000000000
000000000000000000000000000000000000000000000000000000
000000000000000000000000000000000000000000000000000000
000000000000000000000000000000000000000000000000000000
000000000000000000000000000000000000000000000000000000
000000000000000000000000000000000000000000000000000000
000000000000000000000000000000000000000000000000000000
000000000000000000000000000000000000000000000000000000
000000000000000000000000000000000000000000000000000000
000000000000000000000000000000000000000000000000000000
000000000000000000000000000000000000000000000000000000
000000000000000000000000000000000000000000000000000000
000000000000000000000000000000000000000000000000000000

000000000000000000000000000000000000000000000000000000
000000000000000000000000000000000000000000000000000000
000000000000000000000000000000000000000000000000000000
000000000000000000000000000000000000000000000000000000
000000000000000000000000000000000000000000000000000000
000000000000000000000000000000000000000000000000000000
000000000000000000000000000000000000000000000000000000
000000000000000000000000000000000000000000000000000000
000000000000000000000000000000000000000000000000000000
000000000000000000000000000000000000000000000000000000
000000000000000000000000000000000000000000000000000000
000000000000000000000000000000000000000000000000000000
000000000000000000000000000000000000000000000000000000
000000000000000000000000000000000000000000000000000000
000000000000000000000000000000000000000000000000000000
000000000000000000000000000000000000000000000000000000
000000000000000000000000000000000000000000000000000000
000000000000000000000000000000000000000000000000000000
000000000000000000000000000000000000000000000000000000
000000000000000000000000000000000000000000000000000000
000000000000000000000000000000000000000000000000000000
000000000000000000000000000000000000000000000000000000
000000000000000000000000000000000000000000000000000000
000000000000000000000000000000000000000000000000000000
000000000000000000000000000000000000000000000000000000
000000000000000000000000000000000000000000000000000000
000000000000000000000000000000000000000000000000000000
000000000000000000000000000000000000000000000000000000
000000000000000000000000000000000000000000000000000000
000000000000000000000000000000000000000000000000000000
000000000000000000000000000000000000000000000000000000
000000000000000000000000000000000000000000000000000000
000000000000000000000000000000000000000000000000000000
000000000000000000000000000000000000000000000000000000
000000000000000000000000000000000000000000000000000000
000000000000000000000000000000000000000000000000000000
000000000000000000000000000000000000000000000000000000
000000000000000000000000000000000000000000000000000000

0000000000000000000000000000000000000000000000000000
0000000000000000000000000000000000000000000000000000
0000000000000000000000000000000000000000000000000000
0000000000000000000000000000000000000000000000000000
0000000000000000000000000000000000000000000000000000
0000000000000000000000000000000000000000000000000000
0000000000000000000000000000000000000000000000000000
0000000000000000000000000000000000000000000000000000
0000000000000000000000000000000000000000000000000000
0000000000000000000000000000000000000000000000000000
0000000000000000000000000000000000000000000000000000
0000000000000000000000000000000000000000000000000000
0000000000000000000000000000000000000000000000000000
0000000000000000000000000000000000000000000000000000
0000000000000000000000000000000000000000000000000000
0000000000000000000000000000000000000000000000000000
0000000000000000000000000000000000000000000000000000
0000000000000000000000000000000000000000000000000000
0000000000000000000000000000000000000000000000000000
0000000000000000000000000000000000000000000000000000
0000000000000000000000000000000000000000000000000000
0000000000000000000000000000000000000000000000000000
0000000000000000000000000000000000000000000000000000
0000000000000000000000000000000000000000000000000000
0000000000000000000000000000000000000000000000000000
0000000000000000000000000000000000000000000000000000
0000000000000000000000000000000000000000000000000000
0000000000000000000000000000000000000000000000000000
0000000000000000000000000000000000000000000000000000
0000000000000000000000000000000000000000000000000000
0000000000000000000000000000000000000000000000000000
0000000000000000000000000000000000000000000000000000
0000000000000000000000000000000000000000000000000000
0000000000000000000000000000000000000000000000000000
0000000000000000000000000000000000000000000000000000
0000000000000000000000000000000000000000000000000000

00000000000000000000000000000000000000000000000000
00000000000000000000000000000000000000000000000000
00000000000000000000000000000000000000000000000000
00000000000000000000000000000000000000000000000000
00000000000000000000000000000000000000000000000000
00000000000000000000000000000000000000000000000000
00000000000000000000000000000000000000000000000000
00000000000000000000000000000000000000000000000000
00000000000000000000000000000000000000000000000000
00000000000000000000000000000000000000000000000000
00000000000000000000000000000000000000000000000000
00000000000000000000000000000000000000000000000000
00000000000000000000000000000000000000000000000000
00000000000000000000000000000000000000000000000000
00000000000000000000000000000000000000000000000000
00000000000000000000000000000000000000000000000000
00000000000000000000000000000000000000000000000000
00000000000000000000000000000000000000000000000000
00000000000000000000000000000000000000000000000000
00000000000000000000000000000000000000000000000000
00000000000000000000000000000000000000000000000000
00000000000000000000000000000000000000000000000000
00000000000000000000000000000000000000000000000000
00000000000000000000000000000000000000000000000000
00000000000000000000000000000000000000000000000000
00000000000000000000000000000000000000000000000000
00000000000000000000000000000000000000000000000000
00000000000000000000000000000000000000000000000000
000000000000000000000000000000000000000000000God
00000000000000000000000000000000000000000000000000
00000000000000000000000000000000000000000000000000
00000000000000000000000000000000000000000000000000
00000000000000000000000000000000000000000000000000
00000000000000000000000000000000000000000000000000
00000000000000000000000000000000000000000000000000

DR. JAMES KINDLUND

00000000000000000000000000000000000000000000000000
00000000000000000000000000000000000000000000000000
00000000000000000000000000000000000000000000000000
00000000000000000000000000000000000000000000000000
00000000000000000000000000000000000000000000000000
00000000000000000000000000000000000000000000000000
00000000000000000000000000000000000000000000000000
00000000000000000000000000000000000000000000000000
00000000000000000000000000000000000000000000000000
00000000000000000000000000000000000000000000000000
00000000000000000000000000000000000000000000000000
00000000000000000000000000000000000000000000000000
00000000000000000000000000000000000000000000000000
00000000000000000000000000000000000000000000000000
00000000000000000000000000000000000000000000000000
00000000000000000000000000000000000000000000000000
00000000000000000000000000000000000000000000000000
00000000000000000000000000000000000000000000000000
00000000000000000000000000000000000000000000000000
00000000000000000000000000000000000000000000000000
00000000000000000000000000000000000000000000000000
00000000000000000000000000000000000000000000000000
00000000000000000000000000000000000000000000000000
00000000000000000000000000000000000000000000000000
00000000000000000000000000000000000000000000000000
00000000000000000000000000000000000000000000000000
00000000000000000000000000000000000000000000000000
00000000000000000000000000000000000000000000000000
00000000000000000000000000000000000000000000000000
00000000000000000000000000000000000000000000000000
00000000000000000000000000000000000000000000000000
00000000000000000000000000000000000000000000000000
00000000000000000000000000000000000000000000000000

0000000000000000000000000000000000000000000000000
0000000000000000000000000000000000000000000000000
0000000000000000000000000000000000000000000000000
0000000000000000000000000000000000000000000000000
0000000000000000000000000000000000000000000000000
0000000000000000000000000000000000000000000000000
0000000000000000000000000000000000000000000000000
0000000000000000000000000000000000000000000000000
0000000000000000000000000000000000000000000000000
0000000000000000000000000000000000000000000000000
0000000000000000000000000000000000000000000000000
0000000000000000000000000000000000000000000000000
0000000000000000000000000000000000000000000000000
0000000000000000000000000000000000000000000000000
0000000000000000000000000000000000000000000000000
0000000000000000000000000000000000000000000000000
0000000000000000000000000000000000000000000000000
0000000000000000000000000000000000000000000000000
0000000000000000000000000000000000000000000000000
0000000000000000000000000000000000000000000000000
0000000000000000000000000000000000000000000000000
0000000000000000000000000000000000000000000000000
0000000000000000000000000000000000000000000000000
0000000000000000000000000000000000000000000000000
0000000000000000000000000000000000000000000000000
0000000000000000000000000000000000000000000000000
0000000000000000000000000000000000000000000000000
0000000000000000000000000000000000000000000000000
0000000000000000000000000000000000000000000000000
0000000000000000000000000000000000000000000000000
0000000000000000000000000000000000000000000000000
0000000000000000000000000000000000000000000000000
0000000000000000000000000000000000000000000000000
0000000000000000000000000000000000000000000000000
0000000000000000000000000000000000000000000000000
0000000000000000000000000000000000000000000000000
0000000000000000000000000000000000000000000000000

DR. JAMES KINDLUND

0000000000000000000000000000000000000000000000000000
0000000000000000000000000000000000000000000000000000
0000000000000000000000000000000000000000000000000000
0000000000000000000000000000000000000000000000000000
0000000000000000000000000000000000000000000000000000
0000000000000000000000000000000000000000000000000000
0000000000000000000000000000000000000000000000000000
0000000000000000000000000000000000000000000000000000
0000000000000000000000000000000000000000000000000000
0000000000000000000000000000000000000000000000000000
0000000000000000000000000000000000000000000000000000
0000000000000000000000000000000000000000000000000000
0000000000000000000000000000000000000000000000000000
0000000000000000000000000000000000000000000000000000
0000000000000000000000000000000000000000000000000000
0000000000000000000000000000000000000000000000000000
0000000000000000000000000000000000000000000000000000
0000000000000000000000000000000000000000000000000000
0000000000000000000000000000000000000000000000000000
0000000000000000000000000000000000000000000000000000
0000000000000000000000000000000000000000000000000000
0000000000000000000000000000000000000000000000000000
0000000000000000000000000000000000000000000000000000
0000000000000000000000000000000000000000000000000000
0000000000000000000000000000000000000000000000000000
0000000000000000000000000000000000000000000000000000
0000000000000000000000000000000000000000000000000000
0000000000000000000000000000000000000000000000000000
0000000000000000000000000000000000000000000000000000
0000000000000000000000000000000000000000000000000000
0000000000000000000000000000000000000000000000000000
0000000000000000000000000000000000000000000000000000
0000000000000000000000000000000000000000000000000000
0000000000000000000000000000000000000000000000000000
0000000000000000000000000000000000000000000000000000

000000000000000000000000000000000000000000000000000000
000000000000000000000000000000000000000000000000000000
000000000000000000000000000000000000000000000000000000
000000000000000000000000000000000000000000000000000000
000000000000000000000000000000000000000000000000000000
000000000000000000000000000000000000000000000000000000
000000000000000000000000000000000000000000000000000000
000000000000000000000000000000000000000000000000000000
000000000000000000000000000000000000000000000000000000
000000000000000000000000000000000000000000000000000000
000000000000000000000000000000000000000000000000000000
000000000000000000000000000000000000000000000000000000
000000000000000000000000000000000000000000000000000000
000000000000000000000000000000000000000000000000000000
000000000000000000000000000000000000000000000000000000
000000000000000000000000000000000000000000000000000000
000000000000000000000000000000000000000000000000000000
000000000000000000000000000000000000000000000000000000
000000000000000000000000000000000000000000000000000000
000000000000000000000000000000000000000000000000000000
000000000000000000000000000000000000000000000000000000
000000000000000000000000000000000000000000000000000000
000000000000000000000000000000000000000000000000000000
000000000000000000000000000000000000000000000000000000
000000000000000000000000000000000000000000000000000000
000000000000000000000000000000000000000000000000000000
000000000000000000000000000000000000000000000000000000
000000000000000000000000000000000000000000000000000000
000000000000000000000000000000000000000000000000000000
000000000000000000000000000000000000000000000000000000
000000000000000000000000000000000000000000000000000000
000000000000000000000000000000000000000000000000000000
000000000000000000000000000000000000000000000000000000
000000000000000000000000000000000000000000000000000000
000000000000000000000000000000000000000000000000000000
000000000000000000000000000000000000000000000000000000
000000000000000000000000000000000000000000000000000000
000000000000000000000000000000000000000000000000000000

DR. JAMES KINDLUND

0000000000000000000000000000000000000000000000000000000000
0000000000000000000000000000000000000000000000000000000000
0000000000000000000000000000000000000000000000000000000000
0000000000000000000000000000000000000000000000000000000000
0000000000000000000000000000000000000000000000000000000000
0000000000000000000000000000000000000000000000000000000000
0000000000000000000000000000000000000000000000000000000000
0000000000000000000000000000000000000000000000000000000000
0000000000000000000000000000000000000000000000000000000000
0000000000000000000000000000000000000000000000000000000000
0000000000000000000000000000000000000000000000000000000000
0000000000000000000000000000000000000000000000000000000000
0000000000000000000000000000000000000000000000000000000000
0000000000000000000000000000000000000000000000000000000000
0000000000000000000000000000000000000000000000000000000000
0000000000000000000000000000000000000000000000000000000000
0000000000000000000000000000000000000000000000000000000000
0000000000000000000000000000000000000000000000000000000000
0000000000000000000000000000000000000000000000000000000000
0000000000000000000000000000000000000000000000000000000000
0000000000000000000000000000000000000000000000000000000000
0000000000000000000000000000000000000000000000000000000000
0000000000000000000000000000000000000000000000000000000000
0000000000000000000000000000000000000000000000000000000000
0000000000000000000000000000000000000000000000000000000000
0000000000000000000000000000000000000000000000000000000000
0000000000000000000000000000000000000000000000000000000000
0000000000000000000000000000000000000000000000000000000000
0000000000000000000000000000000000000000000000000000000000
0000000000000000000000000000000000000000000000000000000000
0000000000000000000000000000000000000000000000000000000000
0000000000000000000000000000000000000000000000000000000000
0000000000000000000000000000000000000000000000000000000000
0000000000000000000000000000000000000000000000000000000000
0000000000000000000000000000000000000000000000000000000000
0000000000000000000000000000000000000000000000000000000000
0000000000000000000000000000000000000000000000000000000000

00000000000000000000000000000000000000000000000000
00000000000000000000000000000000000000000000000000
00000000000000000000000000000000000000000000000000
00000000000000000000000000000000000000000000000000
00000000000000000000000000000000000000000000000000
00000000000000000000000000000000000000000000000000
00000000000000000000000000000000000000000000000000
00000000000000000000000000000000000000000000000000
00000000000000000000000000000000000000000000000000
00000000000000000000000000000000000000000000000000
00000000000000000000000000000000000000000000000000
00000000000000000000000000000000000000000000000000
00000000000000000000000000000000000000000000000000
00000000000000000000000000000000000000000000000000
00000000000000000000000000000000000000000000000000
00000000000000000000000000000000000000000000000000
00000000000000000000000000000000000000000000000000
00000000000000000000000000000000000000000000000000
00000000000000000000000000000000000000000000000000
00000000000000000000000000000000000000000000000000
00000000000000000000000000000000000000000000000000
00000000000000000000000000000000000000000000000000
00000000000000000000000000000000000000000000000000
00000000000000000000000000000000000000000000000000
00000000000000000000000000000000000000000000000000
00000000000000000000000000000000000000000000000000
00000000000000000000000000000000000000000000000000
00000000000000000000000000000000000000000000000000
00000000 (one in $10^{40,000}$).

Epilogue

Studying the Mind of God would be amazing. The argument that intelligent design theory is a boring explanation for the origins and development of life is simply not true and not good scientific reasoning. The thought of a God designing our world and universe inspired our scientist ancestors. I do not claim to have all the answers, but math does not lie. Time is irrelevant to God. He answers to no one and this includes time. Even the atheist Albert Einstein stated time is relative. I believe one can believe that God is the Creator and not have to submit to the idea of a 10,000-year-old planet. Stated similarly, one does not have to say life on Earth is 10,000 years old to agree with intelligent design theory. Design simply implies it takes place before the building occurs, thus the Earth can remain 4.5 billion years old and still involve a designer. Microevolution has been well established, but common ancestry with gradual, intermediate mutations is mathematically impossible without a designer.

As I have demonstrated, creating life is easy, all you need is the perfect size and strength sun, perfectly sized moon, tides, water, but not too much water and in the right spot; perfect sized planet, be in the safe zone of a spiral galaxy, the correct elements, specific aged stars for heavy elements, a liquid mantle of iron forming an electromagnetic field, the correct number of atoms with perfectly matched interactions, the right molecules, the existence and creation of carbon, the correct atmosphere, just the right atmospheric gases, the precise amount of gravity, the bare minimum of hundreds of genes, the bare minimum hundreds of proteins, with a phospholipid bilayer cellular membrane, autonomous energy production, ingestion, digestion, excrement systems, immune system, clotting systems, and reproduction and boom, you get life.

I always love colorful analogies of impossibilities for evolution theory. Imagine the wind on the beach blowing the sand into a fully functioning fancy sports car. Or perhaps a tornado coursing through a junk yard and making a fully functioning 18-wheeled truck. What if I told you that happened? What would you call it? A miracle? A wonder? A phenomenon? Probably. Well, the random evolution and function of the human eye alone is more sophisticated than what this hypothetical wind accomplished.

Charles Darwin once said, "If it could be demonstrated that any complex organ existed which could not possibly have been formed by numerous, successive, slight modifications, my theory would absolutely break down." Atheism and subsequently Darwin's evolution, was born out of the renaissance when science began explaining how the world worked around us rather than religion. The problem is that very few stopped to figure the one who placed all those workings there. And from this anger and anxiety over religion it birthed the religion of atheism. The age of reasoning sought to disprove God's existence, but 21st century science has certainly discovered God. God told Abraham He would make his descendants as numerous as the stars in the sky. There have been an estimated 106 billion people to have ever lived and there are 100 billion+ stars in the Milky Way.

Virtually all of the pioneering natural scientists of the renaissance era were devoutly Christian. Robert Boyle and Sir Isaac Newton regarded atheists as bombastic provocateurs. Society has made the mistake of reducing faith to a list of ethics, stripped of theological mystery. Humans made the grave blunder of combining philosophy with theology, thus detracting from the majesty and mysticism of faith. As feeble humans we use less than twenty percent of our brain mass for thinking and yet believe we can comprehend or explain the mind of God and His existence.

The science and its complexities discussed here have no logical responses from atheist scientists. Rather we are brow beaten and told to look to quotes by famous scientists who happen to be atheist. As if Carl Sagan, who may have used three percent more of his brain than the rest of us, was capable of comprehending the mind of an omniscient God, or at minimum, be able to prove or disprove His existence. Carl Sagan himself calculated the chance at human evolution to be at $10^{-2,000,000,000}$ percent. As stated at the end of chapter six, the true statistical odds of life randomly forming is one in $10^{40,000}$. Yet we are supposed to believe that a single celled organism, such as bacteria, went from being bacteria to all the mammals, reptiles, birds, amphibians, marsupials, fish, and insects in only 4 billion years.

Sir Isaac Newton, father of physics and calculus once said, "So then gravity may put the planets into motion, but without the Divine power it could never put them into such a circulating motion as they have about the sun … and therefore, this as well as other reasons, I am compelled to ascribe the frame of the system to an intelligent Agent … I have explained the phenomena of the heavens and of our sea by the force of gravity, but I have not yet assigned a cause to gravity" and we humans still haven't.

Gravity, creating something from nothing, arranged in perfect order, with its inexplicable transcendence of space and time; affecting every single piece of matter resonates as God-like to me. Couple gravity with the complexities of our universe, planet, and existence, and one can deeply appreciate the graviton of God.

References

Associated Press. "Scientists may have found appendix's purpose". NBC News, 5 October 2007.

Barresi, M. J., & Gilbert, S. F. (2020). *Developmental biology.* New York, NY: Sinauer Associates an imprint of Oxford University Press.

Behe, M. J. (2006). *Darwin's black box: the biochemical challenge to evolution.* New York: Free Press.

Black, R. (2011, August 23). *Species count put at 8.7 million.* Retrieved June 26, 2020, from https://www.bbc.com/news/science-environment-14616161

Cunliffe, V. (1999). *Why snakes don't have legs.* Trends in Genetics, *15*(8), 306. doi:10.1016/s0168-9525(99)01826-0

Dembski, W. Multiple titles. 1999 – 2011.

Dunn, Rob (January 2, 2012). *"Your Appendix Could Save Your Life".* Scientific American.

F. le Noble, V. Fleury, A. Pries, P. Corvol, A. Eichmann, R.S. Reneman, *Control of arterial branching morphogenesis in embryogenesis: go with the flow.* Cardiovascular Research. Volume

65, Issue 3, February 2005, Pages 619–628. doi: 10.1016/j. cardiores.2004.09.018

Gillis, J. P., & Woodward, T. (2002). *Darwinism under the microscope: how recent scientific evidence points to divine design. Lake Mary, FL: Charisma House.*

Goldman, L., Schafer, A. I., & Cecil, R. L. (2020). *Goldman-Cecil medicine* (26th ed., Vol. 1-2). Philadelphia, PA, PA: Elsevier.

Gray, H., & Carter, H. V. (2019). *Grays anatomy* (41st ed.). London: Arcturus.

Hall, J. E., & Guyton, A. C. (2016). *Guyton and Hall textbook of medical physiology* (13th ed.). Philadelphia (PA): Elsevier.

Holy Bible, New International Version. Zondervan Publishing House, 1984.

James JM, Mukouyama YS. Neuronal action on the developing blood vessel pattern. *Semin Cell Dev Biol. 2011;22(9):1019-1027. doi:10.1016/j.semcdb.2011.09.010*

Nishimoto, S., Minguillon, C., Wood, S., & Logan, M. P. (2014). A Combination of Activation and Repression by a Colinear Hox Code Controls Forelimb-Restricted Expression of Tbx5 and Reveals Hox Protein Specificity. *PLoS Genetics, 10*(3). doi:10.1371/journal.pgen.1004245

Randal Bollinger R., Barbas A.S., Bush E.L., Lin S.S., Parker W. (December 2007). "Biofilms in the large bowel suggest an apparent function of the human vermiform appendix". *Journal of Theoretical Biology.* 249 (4): 826–31. doi:10.1016/j. jtbi.2007.08.032. PMID 17936308.

Schroeder, G. L. (2009). *The science of God: the convergence of scientific and biblical wisdom.* New York: Free Press.

Splittgerber, R., & Snell, R. S. (2019). *Snell's clinical neuroanatomy* (8th ed.). Philadelphia, PA: Wolters Kluwer.

Strobel, L., & Vogel, J. (2014). *The case for a Creator: a journalist investigates scientific evidence that points toward God.* Grand Rapids, MI: Zondervan. M.

Tintinalli, J. E., Ma, O. J., Yealy, D. M., Meckler, G. D., Stapczynski, J. S., Cline, D., & Thomas,

S. J. (2020). *Tintinalli's emergency medicine: a comprehensive study guide* (9th ed.). New York: McGraw Hill Education.

Wolchover, N., & Quanta Magazine. (2020, June 15). Why Gravity Is Not Like the Other Forces.

Retrieved June 15, 2020, from https://www.quantamagazine.org/why-gravity-is-not-like-the-other-forces-20200615/

About the Author

Dr. James Kindlund is a doctor of medical science and a clinical anatomist. He achieved his bachelor's degree in biology from the University of Miami and before that served in the United States Marine Corps reserves. He received his master of science in anatomy from Barry University's School of Podiatric Medicine, he then achieved his master of medical science from Nova Southeastern University, and lastly, he achieved his doctor of medical science from Lincoln Memorial University's DeBusk College of Osteopathic Medicine. He has practiced in both internal and emergency medicine at the University of Florida medical system. He has published several, peer-reviewed scientific articles, as well as a medical book chapter.

Printed in the United States
By Bookmasters